# WELLSPRINGS

Including the Richard Ellmann Lectures
in Modern Literature

MARIO VARGAS LLOSA

# WELLSPRINGS

HARVARD UNIVERSITY PRESS

Cambridge, Massachusetts, and London, England

2008

Library of Congress Cataloging-in-Publication Data

Vargas Llosa, Mario, 1936–

Wellsprings / Mario Vargas Llosa.

p.   cm.

ISBN-13: 978-0-674-02836-4

ISBN-10: 0-674-02836-8

1. Spanish American literature—History and criticism.

2. Spanish literature—History and criticism.   I. Title.

PQ7081.V38 2007

860.9—dc22        2007038664

# CONTENTS

# 1

## FOUR CENTURIES OF
## DON QUIXOTE

The plethora of works on Cervantes, and the official worship that he receives, have fossilized him to some extent, turning him into a symbol of a language and a culture, as has happened with Homer, Dante, and Shakespeare. It is easy to forget, in the midst of all this critical acclaim, that Cervantes was a person like all of us, faced with the pitfalls of an uncertain destiny, whose work was not conceived miraculously or by chance but was achieved through determination, hard work, craftsmanship, and patience.

In none of these other authors is the refreshing humanity of the common man as evident as in the eventful life that began one autumn day in 1547 in Alcalá de Henares. Despite the perseverance of historians, the life of Miguel de Cervantes Saavedra, like that of Shakespeare, still has large shadowy, unexplored areas. We know that Miguel was a Spanish citizen without title or fortune, who lived modestly and in dire straits. His father, Rodrigo Cervantes—a barber and unskilled surgeon whose day-to-day existence was plagued by disputes and bad luck—probably bequeathed only misfortunes, lawsuits, excommunications, evasions, and tight spots to his son.

The two harquebus wounds Miguel received in Lepanto and the resulting paralysis of his left hand have led hagiographers to turn him into a hero. But he was no hero, at least not in the epic sense of the word, only in that other, more modest sense, which is the heroism of nameless people who resist frequent setbacks and troubles without giving up. He was tried in absentia for wounding Antonio de Sigura and subsequently escaped to Italy. He endured five years of imprisonment in Algiers and near slavery at the hands of the renegade Greek Dali Mami. Officials refused to allow him to serve the Crown in the Indies, and at one point he was jailed for debts and alleged trafficking. Widespread rumors circulated about the transgressions of his sisters and his illegitimate daughter, Isabel. But beyond all this, there was the bitterness he felt at not having achieved glory in poetry, the princely genre, and at having to content himself instead with plebian prose, so distant from the intellectual elite and so close to the masses.

The life of Cervantes moves and saddens us, but it does not elicit our admiration: it was the precarious life of an ordinary Spaniard during times of upheaval. What baffles us is how this life, marked by sordidness, suffering, and frustration, could have produced an adventure as generous as *Don Quixote*—that healthy, cheerful depiction of the human condition. It might seem that everything has already been said about this subject; yet every time we reread the novel and confirm how vibrant and current it remains, we discover, yet again, that there will always be new things to say.

All works of genius are both obvious and enigmatic. *Don Quixote*, like the *Odyssey*, the *Divine Comedy*, or *Hamlet*, enriches us as human beings, demonstrating that through artistic creation men and women can break through the limits of their condition and achieve a type of immortality. At the same time, *Don Quixote* devastates us, making us aware of our smallness when compared with the giant who conceived that great endeavor. How could Cervantes perpetrate such a deicide? How was it possible to thus defy the creation of the Creator? By writing the story of the ingenious hidalgo, Cervantes took the Spanish language to unprecedented heights and established an emblematic ceiling for those of us who write in that language. And he renovated the genre of the novel, giving it a complexity and subtleness as vast as the destructive and reconstructive ambitions of the world that brings it to life. From then on, it would become the yardstick by which all novels were measured, in the same way that all theater secretly glances at Shakespeare's plays, the cornerstone of the stage.

That *Don Quixote* is both a great comedy and a very serious novel, that it recreates in a simple myth the insoluble dialectic between the real and the ideal, and that it undermines the novels of chivalry while paying them homage have been explained to us by the critics. However, they have not often mentioned that among the many things it is, *Don Quixote,* like all great literary paradigms, is also a fiction about fiction, about what fiction is and how it operates in life, the service it provides and the havoc it can cause. This idea reappears in all literary fiction because it is an ongoing theme in the lives not just of writers but of people in general. No novelist expressed this idea as astutely, seductively, and clearly as Cervantes did, without meaning to or even knowing he was doing so, in a novel that he conceived as a simple criticism of a literary trend.

The origin of fiction must have been quite simple, although it later became complicated. Men and women, for the most part, are not satisfied with the lives they lead and find their aspirations perpetually beyond reach. Since they refuse to resign themselves to the realities of their existence, they live in dreams—in the stories they tell. The task of inventing and telling stories to make existence more tolerable is as ancient as language itself. It has undoubtedly been practiced since the first signs of intelligent communication replaced the grunts and leaps of our primitive ancestors. Sitting near the fire in their protective caves, these protohumans must have listened to the first works of fiction with reverence, just as, through the millennia and across the globe, children have soaked up their grandmothers' tales, tribes have incorporated the myths of their shamans, villagers have welcomed their traveling minstrels, and the powerful in salons and palaces have rewarded their balladeers.

Literature is just one recent branch of this opulent tree we call fiction. Writing established what was until then a perishable universe of oral tradition, stabilizing it and giving permanence to its myths and archetypes. Thanks to writing, in some mysterious way, alternative lives created to fill the gap between reality and desire obtained the right to citizenship, and the ghosts of imagination became part of life experience, forming, in the words of Balzac, the private history of nations.

Fiction is entertainment only in the second or third instance, although it is nothing if it is not also fun and magical. While the turn to fiction is, first, an act of rebellion against the limitations of real life, it is also a compensation for those who are uneasy living in the prison of a single destiny, those who are drawn to that "temptation of the impossible" which, according to Lamartine, made the creation of Victor Hugo's *Les Misérables* possible. Individuals who create and enjoy fiction want to step out of their lives in order to play a leading role in others richer or more sordid, purer or more terrible, than those they were destined to live.

This way of explaining the attractions of fiction may seem rather grim, because at first glance it seems no more than the harmless pastime of a person who, in the evenings before he nods off, commits Raskolnikov's crime and then falls asleep, or of a virtuous lady who, along with her five o'clock tea, takes part in the antics of Boccaccio's women without her husband's knowledge. However, as Alonso Quijano reveals, fiction is something more than simply a way to avoid boredom. It provides a transitory relief from an existential discontent; it feeds our hunger for something different from what we are and what we have. And yet, paradoxically, fiction exacerbates as well as placates that primal urge. The borrowed

lives that are ours thanks to fiction, rather than sati-
ating our desires, increase them and make us more
aware of how small we are compared with the extraordinary beings conjured by the fantasist lurking
within us.

Fiction is both a testament to and a source of our
nonconformity. Contemptuous of the world as it is,
fiction is irrefutable proof that reality—life lived—is
tailored only to what we are, not to what we wish to
be. The fictitious life we superimpose onto real life is
not a tribute to social harmony but just the opposite,
especially if it is produced in times of upheaval, as
was the case when Cervantes wrote his jovial epic.
Why would a society foster these parallel lives, these
lies, if what it had was already enough, if the truths
of its existence were sufficient? The appearance of a
great novel is always a sign of a vital rebelliousness
taking the shape of a fictional world—one which,
while resembling the real world, actually questions
or rejects it. That may explain the fortitude with
which Cervantes appears to have endured his difficult circumstances: by taking revenge on them
through a symbolic deicide, he replaced the reality
that mistreated him with the splendor which, draw-
ing strength from his disappointments, he invented
to oppose it.

Fighting reality with fantasy, which is what we do

when we tell or invent stories, is an amusing pastime as long as we remain clear about the insurmountable barriers between fiction and reality. When that barrier is breached and the two worlds collide, as happens in the mind of Alonso Quijano, the game gives way to madness and can take a tragic turn. Although the reckless man of La Mancha undertakes innumerable foolish adventures, since he acts according to the perceptions of an essentially false reality, or rather, one falsified by chivalrous fiction, his eccentricities have never met with the disdain of readers. To the contrary, even for his contemporaries, who roared with laughter as they read what they viewed as a comic novel, the gaunt man of La Mancha who attacked windmills believing them to be giants, mistook the barber's shaving bowl for Mambrino's helmet, and saw castles and palaces in roadside inns appears as a morally superior individual pursuing a noble, idealistic adventure, even though unbridled fantasy clouds his reason, causing everything to turn out wrong.

From the beginning, readers have identified with Don Quixote, who succumbs to the temptation of the impossible—trying to live a fiction—and have kept their distance from Sancho Panza, who remains walled in by the possible—a man whose material concerns suffocate his spirit and whose horizons are limited by his excessive pragmatism. At first glance, this unequal appraisal of the celebrated pair is unfair, at least when the viewpoint shifts from the individual to the larger society. Clearly, Don Quixote's rejection of the world as it is creates many messy situations, violent acts, and even catastrophes: the pair destroy the possessions of others, free dangerous criminals, decimate flocks, terrify humble villagers, or leave them beaten and robbed.

Moreover, although the comic slant of Don Quixote's adventures and the beatings and abuse he usually receives soften this aspect of him, there is a feature of his personality which, outside the realm of fiction, is troubling: Don Quixote is a fanatic. He has the one-sided vision of the dogmatic believer, the absolute owner of the truth, incapable of learning from his mistakes, having doubts, or accepting that reason and intelligence are sometimes better tools for understanding reality than are faith and passion. He is never wrong. When Sancho tries to make him see that the enemies he attacked were merely goatskin wine bags, or a flock of goats, or simple pilgrims or shepherds, he berates his squire. No, that is not how it was: magicians like the clever Freston twisted reality to make it hurt and ridicule him. These sorcerers can fantastically transform the real world without in the least affecting Quixote's certainty of being right and just, leading him to thrust his lance into the ghosts with which his raging fantasy has populated the world.

The character makes us laugh, and yet he completely lacks a sense of humor. Like all absolute believers, he is deadly serious. His misadventures move us because everything turns out badly, and especially because what he does and suffers happens out there, far from us, in fiction. Don Quixote's madness is a presentiment of things to come and also contains a frontal attack on the prejudices that madness causes. Cervantes managed to sketch not only the outline of a provincial hidalgo pining for the bygone era of knights errant but also a prototype of another form of pernicious madness or mental unreality. In his own time, this madness was embodied in the inquisitors who burned infidels, and before them were the crusaders who preached and practiced holy war. Later it would be the Jacobean worshippers of the goddess of Reason who burned churches and beheaded priests and nuns, then the Aryans who would exterminate "inferior" races in Nazi concentration camps, and the commissars who, in defense of ideological orthodoxy, would make millions of real or alleged dissidents disappear in the Siberian gulag.

Quixote's adventures are only agreeable for his readers, never for those poor souls who in his imagination are transformed into magicians, enchanted people, and knights errant, whom he frequently tries to attack with his lance. By contrast, the novel seeks to introduce Sancho Panza as a coarse illiterate who seems to have no greater ambition in life than to fill his stomach. Although from an individual standpoint he appears as a rough-hewn, foolish materialist, from a social point of view he is a citizen much more respectful of the law and of his neighbor than is his master. He is not as cultured because he does not know how to read or write, but he is blessed with an immense natural wisdom, honed in the tough school of survival. He drinks from an inexhaustible wellspring of refrains, sayings, and phrases of popular culture to explain to his master, and to himself, the calamities that Don Quixote has dragged him into. Unlike Don Quixote, who never changes from a man armor-plated by his unyielding convictions except when he recovers his sanity at the end of the story, Sancho Panza, despite his ignorance, is an open spirit, whose life experiences transform him.

The Sancho Panza we see in the kingdom of the dukes, delighting the duchess with his loquaciousness and earthy philosophy and governing Barataria Island with Solomonic prudence, has little in common with the boor he was when Alonso Quijano enlisted him for his knightly adventure. Unlike Don

Quixote, Sancho conforms to the possible, and for that reason he is happier, or rather less unhappy, than the ingenious hidalgo, condemned to misery by his perpetual dissatisfaction with the world as it is. In his own way, Don Quixote, the quintessential dissident, is a hero; and in his own way, the pragmatic Sancho is the ideal citizen, whose behavior guarantees the social order, although not always freedom or progress. If Sancho's pragmatism and understanding of the real things of this world had prevailed, Don Quixote would have been less battered and would have had more teeth in his mouth at the end of the story. But then there would have been no novel—or it would have been deadly boring—and Spanish language and literature would have been less fertile than they are.

Don Quixote without Sancho Panza, his squire, is incomplete—we might go so far as to say he only partially exists. His companion in his adventures completes him and vice versa. They could not be more dissimilar. One is frail, lanky, skeletal, tortured by a burning illusion that clouds, and sometimes abolishes, reality; the other is stocky, beer-bellied, materialistic, and practical to an extreme. Why do they seem to us inseparable, two sides of a single being? Because, intertwined, what in each of them is caricatural and exaggerated disappears, and normality emerges. The ambiguous, complex view of humanity that informs Quixote's actions would not be apparent without the strong mutual dependence of this mismatched pair joined together by fiction.

Sancho Panza is Don Quixote's anchor; without him, the man of La Mancha would escape the bonds of gravity and float to such heights that he would eventually disappear. Without Sancho, Don Quixote would dissolve upon contact with reality, in the way that mirages dissolve with the approach of the observer. But thanks to Sancho, the chimeras and fantasies of Don Quixote have an earthly, rational counterweight that saves the hero from disintegration. And thanks to Don Quixote, his squire—intrigued, fascinated, and admiring of a master whose insanities he does not completely understand—lives more fully, acquiring a sheen of eccentricity and even an aura of spirituality, despite his pigheaded talent for submission and groveling.

At the end of the second part of *Don Quixote,* a strange role reversal takes place. Sancho Panza, possessed by his master's appetite for unreality, urges him to rise from his deathbed, refuse realism, and go out with him and live out a new fantasy, this time not chivalrous but pastoral. Quixote, who by this time has recovered his sanity and rejected imaginative delirium, resigns himself to the objective, conformist vision of the world that belonged to Sancho at the beginning of the story.

All of this means at least two things. First, we do

not admire Quixote as a real person but rather as a specter, a fictional character, and we feel alienated from Sancho precisely because, unlike his master, he is so similar to us. For this reason, his actions and views do not resemble those of a character from a novel but rather those of a mere mortal. This leads to a second conclusion: that fiction exists not to represent reality but to negate it, to transmute it into an unreality, which—when the novelist masters the verbal sleight of hand as Cervantes did—appears to us as authentic, when it is actually reality's antithesis.

Perhaps this is the symbolism of Quixote that most intimately arouses our sympathy toward this ungainly figure. He has converted into a daily practice the magic that common mortals also need to fill life's voids but use only sporadically, when they dream, read, or go to the theater—that is, when they become other people in their imagination. Don Quixote does not become someone else merely in his imagination: he actually leaves himself, crosses forbidden limits toward the mirages of fiction, and not even the worst misfortunes manage to return him to the real world. More than the content of his dreams or his set of values, what in him is eternal is his hunger for fiction, which gnaws away at him and is so overpowering that it pushes him to make an absurd trade: to give up being flesh and blood in exchange for becoming a chimera, an illusion.

This quixotic enterprise—to leave reality in an attempt to experience fantasy—has produced exceptional individuals whose eccentricities have contributed to the world's store of knowledge and without which life would be even grayer than it already is. Scientific, social, economic, and cultural progress is due to impulsive visionaries like Alonso Quijano. Without them, Europe would not have discovered America, or the printing press, or human rights, and we would continue to dance around in circles, as the Iroquois once did, to make rain fall on the crops. Yet it is also true that the call of the unreal, by awakening in men and women an appetite for what they do not and will never have, has greatly contributed to human unhappiness. It is a paradox, since there is no way realistically to do what Quixote attempts, which is to live simultaneously in the objective life of history and the subjective life of fiction.

Of course, Cervantes and his readers have agreed upon a figurative way to resolve this problem. The novel depends on a subconscious contract with the public that allows the novelist to play the liar. The novel is a genre of extended storytelling created to complete the incomplete lives of mortals by supplying, on a large canvas, the heroism, passion, intelligence, or terror they long for but do not have, or at least not to the extent demanded by imagination— which is the engine that fuels our dissidence with life. True, novels and other forms of fiction are fleeting palliatives for the disquiet arising from an awareness of our limitations, from the impossibility of being and doing all that our imagination and desires demand. But, even so, fiction enables us to live multiple lives in a universe of shadows which, though fragile and slight, we incorporate into our lives. These ghosts influence our destinies and help us to resolve the conflict resulting from our strange condition of having a body condemned to a single life and appetites demanding another thousand. To tell stories is to live more, and better.

Literature influences life in mysterious ways, of course, and all that is said on this matter should be taken with caution. Did fiction make Don Alonso Quijano more miserable or happier? On the one hand, it pitted him against the world, led him to crash head-on against stubborn reality, and caused him to be defeated in every battle. On the other, did he not live more fully than his peers? Would his fate have been more enviable if he had not obstinately projected onto real life the creatures of his spirit? Is there not, in his foolish enterprise, something that redeems him, and us, from crushing routine?

While all people who resort to fiction have a particular devotion to Don Quixote, those of us who dedicate our lives to writing fiction feel deeply affected by his story. It symbolizes what we embark on each time we face a blank page. We emulate Don Quixote as we undertake the task of finding fantastic images and words to root the imaginary in daily life, illusion in action, myth in history. We find in his adventure incentives for our own.

Cervantes was one of the first writers to use fiction itself to describe the function of fiction in life. He showed how life and literary fiction, being essentially distinct, complement, influence, and enrich one another, and how fiction enables individuals to break through the incarcerating limits of their individuality and multiply their particular destinies. Alonso Quijano represents the extreme, deluded way of embarking on a constant search for the richer, more varied lives that human beings undertake through fiction; he has gone much further than most readers or listeners of stories, who shift back and forth from the real world to literary fantasies in an effort to escape the oppression of the mundane.

*Don Quixote* is a novel told not only by Cervantes and Cide Hamete Benengeli, the purported writer in Arabic of the original manuscript that he adapted and transcribed into Spanish, but also by characters in the novel itself, who create a tangled jungle of stories. In this fictional world, most men and women exercise their passion for storytelling, by embellishing, exaggerating, or distorting the real world through the word. It is a contagious passion. At the beginning of the novel, only the deluded Alonso Quijano manifests it. But later, this tendency to project oneself through fiction spreads throughout his environment.

Thus, for example, to lure Quixote back to the village, the priest and barber invent a story, with the aid of Dorotea, the woman jilted by Fernando. Shortly thereafter, we see everyone—priest, barber, Sancho Panza, Dorotea, Cardenio—living out the fiction they have invented, in the same way that Don Quixote experiences his world of knights errant and magicians. This process intensifies, reaching its climax in the second part of the novel when Quixote and Sancho are staying in the land of the mysterious duke and duchess. Seduced by the adventures of the ingenious hidalgo, which they have read about in the first part of the story, the duke stages a series of representations—the adventure with Clavileño, the flying horse, and Sancho's governance of Barataria Island—that transforms life into fiction. Thus, although Don Quixote is always defeated in his concrete adventures, the novel compensates him for his quests because his delirious obsession—to convert lived reality into the fictional reality of the novels of chivalry—gradually permeates the whole of life, transforming it into theater, literature, and invention.

In terms of the Spanish language, *Don Quixote* is the paradigmatic work of literature, the novel that most brilliantly captures the imaginary life that fiction represents, inspired by the real but essentially distinct from it. Why do certain books, such as *Don Quixote* and the *Divine Comedy,* or authors such as Shakespeare and Goethe, become emblems of a civilization?

The first reason is linguistic. In *Don Quixote,* the Spanish language reaches its maximum expression and lavishly displays its formidable powers. It reveals its diversity and capacity to articulate a wide range of states and feelings, humor, drama, and irony, to translate into words exterior and interior landscapes, and to show, by qualifying or naming them, the infinite shades of human experience. In certain pages of *Don Quixote,* Spanish becomes music; in others, dreams; in still others, phantasmagoria; and frequently, crude and brutal reality.

In much of the novel, language is a game, an intellectual juggling act. To speak about *one* language in *Don Quixote* is to oversimplify because, in truth, its pages are filled with a variety of languages, distinct but at the same time solidly joined at their roots, like the offspring of a single organism. There is the archaic, engulfing, and ingenious language that Don Quixote of La Mancha uses, inspired by what the books of chivalry attribute to knights errant—a language which in Cervantes' novel is both parody and homage. At the other extreme, there is the popular, coarse language of Sancho Panza, brimming with refrains and sayings lifted from street talk, from the common people, a flavorful, vital, picturesque, and effervescent language. And there is a refined literary language, carefully wrought and much less personalized than that used by Don Quixote and his squire, which Cervantes often employs to narrate the autonomous stories incorporated into the novel—stories that serve to expand the tale of the hidalgo from La Mancha, bringing in references to a historical past and to other imaginative worlds and revealing the universal nature of the text. Yet, despite this profusion of styles, when reading *Don Quixote* the reader always has the sense of a seamless unit, of a single language displaying its metamorphoses in this story, thanks to the expert hand that governs its luxuriant prose.

Of course, the power and elegance, subtlety and variety of Cervantes' prose, which bewitches, woos, and envelopes us in a world of fiction, is one of the reasons why *Don Quixote* is *the* symbolic book of the Spanish language. This language also wields its power in other extraordinary classics, such as the dialogues of *La Celestina* or the poems of Góngora and Quevedo. However, these works, despite their genius, have never been seen as exemplary the way *Don Quixote* has. Why? Because *Don Quixote* immortalized a pair, Sancho Panza and Don Quixote, with whom readers from all eras and cultures could identify, and in whom they could recognize something profound and permanent.

This identification has to do with the boundless ambition of the work—a pristine example of the total novel—and with the conviction, maintained by generations of readers, that the vicissitudes and characters of Cervantes' novel captured the essence of a people, their idiosyncrasies, characteristic features and values, their particular history and spiritual concerns—in sum, all that gives a society a unique, individual shape. It does not matter that this idea turns out to be false when subjected to scientific scrutiny, since, no matter how cohesive and sovereign a community is and has been, no human group is so homogenous that it can be embodied in a single work, in a single actor, even in that of an author as prolific as Shakespeare. However, we are not talking now about an objective phenomenon but rather a myth. Myth is a gradual, mysterious choice people make of models, icons, prototypes, and symbols to represent themselves, extracted from the wellsprings of folklore, religion, and literature. Through four centuries of history, dozens of generations of Spanish speakers have decided that *Don Quixote* expresses and represents us, what we are, what we speak, what we create and believe in, more intensely, beautifully, and faithfully than any other literary creation.

This reveals something about both Spanish speakers and *Don Quixote*. To investigate further, we must take a close look at the word bequeathed to us by Cervantes' character: quixotic. It means audacious, effusive, idealistic, visionary, and heroic. But also meddlesome, humorless, and suspicious of reality. So it seems this is what we would like to be. Who in Spain or Latin America would venture to deny this, in light of the clear proof we have frequently given in history of our lack of realism, of our divorce from the objective world, of that excessive dependence on ideals that characterizes *Don Quixote*?

Is this a defect or a virtue? It depends on the prism through which we view it. From a certain standpoint, attacking windmills mistakenly taken for giants could be an admirable undertaking, if we see it as the result of a dissatisfaction with the narrow confines of reality that provokes in nonconformist spirits a desire to enrich life—that is, if we see it as the refusal of the rebellious to yield to a pedestrian existence. However, it is also possible to define that attitude as a form of profound alienation which prevents people from fully judging the world or understanding historical events, making these individuals incapable of distinguishing between reality and nonreality and causing them—rather like children—to act in an imprudent, irresponsible, and catastrophic manner, creating havoc in themselves and their social environment.

In *Don Quixote,* these contradictory interpretations are inseparable, coinciding in a single and therefore ambiguous personality—which is to say, a profoundly human one, since the most typical human characteristic is ambiguity. Unlike chivalric heroes such as Amadis of Gaul, Tristan de Leonis, or Esplandian, whose models are flat, rectilinear figures, without nuance, Don Quixote is split by a complexity that makes him susceptible to contradictory interpretations, like any flesh and blood mortal. The humanity of Cervantes' character places him far above his chivalric peers and confers on him the condition of the first hero of the modern novel.

In addition to being ambiguous, Don Quixote is a free individual. He practices freedom in all acts without the least concern for what risks this may entail, convinced that "Freedom, Sancho, is one of the most precious gifts bestowed by heaven on man; no treasures that the earth contains and the sea conceals can compare with it; for freedom, as for honor, men can and should risk their lives and, in contrast, captivity is the worst evil that can befall them" (vol. 2, chap. 58). This beautiful definition of freedom is that of a recalcitrant individualist and an insolent libertarian. Quixote, unlike the respectful Sancho, who is fearful of authority and the law, believes that justice in this world is not something to be administered by the state—a remote and abstract entity whose existence he does not even notice.

Justice is, rather, the work of idealistic, honest citizens like himself and his kind, the knights errant who set out "for the service of their republic" and take on their shoulders the task of "righting wrongs, offering succor to widows, and protecting damsels" (vol. 2, chap. 9), along with defending the needy. His idea of justice is not subordinated to secular or religious law. It obeys a strong, personal conception, which he puts into practice even though it sends him on a collision course with the established order—for example, when, in the name of his immense love of freedom, he frees twelve galley slaves, among them the fierce Ginés de Pasamonte. Madness and humor attenuate but do not extinguish Quixote's penchant for rebelling against, upsetting, and subverting the established order. For better or worse, this penchant is also a reflection of ourselves, and has been nothing less than a constant in the history of Latin America.

We can draw innumerable ideas and lessons from this novel, which is now four centuries old. However, its most magical and enduring feature continues to be that odd pair riding through its pages, browbeaten, absurd, colorful, funny, tender, moving, indefatigable, who reveal to us, with each adventure, the marvelous abundance of the imagination in re-creating human lives.

# 2

## THE FICTIONS OF BORGES

When I was a student, I had a passion for Sartre, and I firmly believed in his notion that the writer's commitment was to his own times and to the society in which he lived, that "words were actions," and that through writing a man or woman could influence history. Today, such ideas seem naive and even tedious—we live in an age of smug skepticism about the power of literature as well as history—but in the 1950s the notion that the world could be changed for the better, and that literature should contribute to this, struck many of us as both persuasive and exciting.

By then, Borges' influence was beginning to be felt beyond the small circle of admirers who read his work in the Argentine literary magazine *Sur*. In a number of Latin American cities, ardent followers fought over the rare editions of his books as if they were treasure and learned by heart those visionary random lists, or catalogues, that inhabit Borges' pages—the particularly beautiful one from "The Aleph," for instance—and tried to incorporate in their work not only his labyrinths, tigers, mirrors, masks, and knives but also his strikingly original use of adjectives and adverbs.

In Lima, the first of these Borges enthusiasts I came across was a friend and contemporary with whom I shared my books and literary dreams. Borges was always an inexhaustible topic of discussion. In a clinically pure way, he stood for everything Sartre had taught me to hate: the artist retreating from the world around him to take refuge in a world of intellect, erudition, and fantasy; the writer looking down on politics, history, and day-to-day reality, while shamelessly displaying his skepticism and wry disdain for everything that was not literature; the intellectual who not only allowed himself to treat ironically the dogmas and utopias of the left but who took his own iconoclasm to the extreme of joining the Conservative Party and breezily justifying this move by claiming that gentlemen prefer lost causes.

In our discussions, I tried to show with all the Sartrean malice I could command that an intellectual who wrote, spoke, and behaved the way Borges did somehow shared responsibility for all the world's social ills. That his stories and poems were little more than *bibelots d'inanité sonore,* mere trinkets of high-sounding emptiness, and that History with its terrible sense of justice—which progressives wield, as it suits them, like an executioner's ax or a gambler's marked card—would one day give him his just deserts. But once the arguments were over, in the solitude of my room or the library—like the fanatical puritan of Somerset Maugham's *Rain,* who gives in to the temptation of the flesh he renounces—I found Borges' spell irresistible. I would read his stories, poems, and essays in utter amazement; and the adulterous feeling I had that I was betraying my mentor Sartre added a perverse pleasure.

I have been somewhat fickle in my literary passions; and nowadays when I reread many of the writers who were once my models, especially during adolescence, I find them boring—Sartre included. But the secret, sinful passion I harbored for Borges' work has never faded, and rereading him, which I have done from time to time like a believer performing a sacred ritual, has always been a happy experience. Only recently, I read all his work again, one piece after the other, and once more I marveled—exactly as I had done the first time—at his elegant and limpid prose, the refinement of his stories, the excellence of his craftsmanship. I am quite aware of how ephemeral literary assessments can be, but in Borges' case we can quite justifiably state that he is the most important thing to happen to imaginative writing in the Spanish language in modern times, and one of the most memorable artists of our age.

I also believe that the debt we who write in Spanish owe to Borges is enormous. That includes even those of us, like myself, who have never written a story of pure fantasy or felt any particular affinity with ghosts and doubles, with the infinite, or with the metaphysics of Schopenhauer. For Latin American writers, Borges heralded the end of a kind of inferiority complex that inhibited us, unwittingly of course, from broaching certain subjects and that kept us imprisoned in a provincial outlook. Before Borges, it seemed a piece of foolhardiness or self-delusion for one of us to feel at home in a larger world culture, in the way that a European or a North American might.

A handful of Latin America *modernista* poets had previously done so, of course, but their attempts—even in the case of the most famous among them, Rubén Darío—smacked of pastiche or whimsicality, something akin to a superficial, slightly frivolous journey through a foreign land. Latin American writers had forgotten what our classical writers like Inca Gar-

cilaso or Sor Juana Inés de la Cruz never doubted—
that through language and history they were part
and parcel of Western culture, not mere amanuenses
or colonials but a legitimate part of that tradition,
ever since Spaniards and Portuguese, four and a half
centuries earlier, extended the frontiers of Western
culture to the southern hemisphere. With Borges,
this engagement became possible once more. But at
the same time, Borges' work was proof that being
part of this broader cultural history took nothing
away from a Latin American writer's sovereignty or
originality.

Few European writers have assimilated the legacy
of the West as completely and thoroughly as this
poet and storyteller from the periphery. Who among
Borges' contemporaries handled with such ease Scan-
dinavian myths, Anglo-Saxon poetry, German philosophy, Spain's Golden Age literature, the English poets, Dante, Homer, and the myths and legends of the
Far and Middle East that Europeans translated and
gave to the world? But this did not make Borges European. I remember the surprise of my students at
Queen Mary College in the University of London
during the 1960s—we were reading *Ficciones* and *El
Aleph*—when I told them that some Latin Americans
accused Borges of being Europeanized, of being little more than an English writer. They could not see

why. To them, this writer, in whose stories so many different countries, ages, themes, and cultural references are intertwined, seemed as exotic as the cha-cha-cha, which was all the rage at the time. They were not wrong. Borges was not a writer imprisoned within national tradition, as European writers often are, and this facilitated his journeys through cultural space, in which, thanks to the many languages he knew, he moved with consummate ease.

This cosmopolitanism, this eagerness to be a master of such a far-ranging cultural sphere, this desire to invent a past for oneself in dialogue with the outside, was a way of being profoundly Argentine—which is to say, Latin American. But in Borges' case, his intense involvement with European literature was also a way of shaping his own personal geography, a way of being Borges. Through his broad interests and his private demons he was weaving a fabric of great originality, made up of strange combinations in which the prose of Stevenson and *The Arabian Nights,* translated by Englishmen and Frenchmen, appear alongside gauchos out of *Martín Fierro* and characters from Icelandic sagas, and in which two old-time hoodlums, from a Buenos Aires more imagined than remembered, fight with knives in a quarrel which seems like the extension of a medieval dispute that results in death by fire of two Chris-

tian theologians. Against the unique Borgesian backdrop, the most heterogeneous creatures and events
parade—just as they do, in "The Aleph," in Carlos
Argentino Daneri's cellar. But in contrast to what
takes place on that tiny passive screen, which can reveal the elements of the universe only at random,
in Borges' work every element and every being is
brought together, filtered through a single point of
view, and given individual character through verbal
expression.

Here is another area in which Latin American
writers owe much to the example of Borges. Not
only did he prove to us that an Argentine could speak
with authority on Shakespeare and create convincing
stories set in Aberdeen, but he also revolutionized
the tradition of his literary language. Note that I said
"example" and not "influence." To the extent that
Borges' prose has been "influential," it has—because
of its wild originality—wreaked havoc among countless admirers, in whose work the use of certain images or verbs or adjectives established by him turns
into mere parody. This is the most readily detect-
able influence, for Borges was one of the writers
who managed completely to put his own personal
stamp on the Spanish language. "Word music" was
his term for it, and it is as distinctive in him as it
is in the most illustrious of our classical writers—

namely, Quevedo, whom Borges admired, and Góngora, whom he did not. Borges' prose is so recognizable to the ear that often in someone else's work a single sentence or even a simple verb (*conjeturar*, for example, or *fatigar* used transitively) becomes a clear giveaway of Borges' influence.

Borges made a profound impression on Spanish literary prose, as before him Rubén Darío had on poetry. The difference between them is that Darío imported and introduced from France a number of mannerisms and themes that he adapted to his own world and to his own idiosyncratic style. To some extent, all this expressed the feelings (and at times the snobbery) of a particular period and a certain social milieu. Which is why his devices could be used by so many without his followers losing their individual voices. The Borges revolution was personal. It represented him alone, and only in a vague, roundabout way was it connected with the setting in which he was formed and which in turn he helped crucially to form—that of the magazine *Sur.* Which is why in anyone else's hands Borges' style comes across as caricature.

But this clearly does not diminish his importance or lessen in the slightest the enormous pleasure his prose gives us. It can be savored, word by word, like a delicacy. What is revolutionary about Borges' prose is that it contains almost as many ideas as words, for his precision and concision are absolute. While this is not uncommon in English or French literature, in Hispanic literature it has few precedents. Marta Pizarro, a character in Borges' story "The Duel," reads Lugones and Ortega y Gasset, and this confirms "her suspicion that the language to which she had been born was less fit for expressing the mind or the passions than for verbal showing off."

Joking aside, if we omit what she says about the passions there is some truth to her remark. Like Italian or Portuguese, Spanish is a wordy language, bountiful and flamboyant, with a formidable emotional range. But for these same reasons it is conceptually inexact. The work of our greatest prose writers, beginning with Cervantes, is like a splendid fireworks display in which every idea is preceded and surrounded by a sumptuous verbal court of servants, suitors, and pages, whose function is purely decorative. Color, temperature, and music are as important in our prose as ideas, and in some cases—Lezama Lima, for example—more so.

There is nothing objectionable about these typically Spanish rhetorical excesses. They profoundly express the nature of a people, a way of being in which the emotional and the concrete prevail over the intellectual and the abstract. This is why Valle-Inclán, Alfonso Reyes, Alejo Carpentier, and Camilo

José Cela—to cite four magnificent prose writers—
are so verbose in their writing. This does not make
their prose either less skillful or more superficial
than that of a Valéry or a T. S. Eliot. They are simply
quite different, just as Latin Americans are different
from the English and the French. To us, ideas are formulated and captured more effectively when fleshed
out with emotion and feeling or in some way incorporated into concrete reality, into life, far more than
they are in a logical discourse. This, perhaps, is why
we have such a rich literature and such a dearth
of philosophers. The most illustrious thinker in the
Spanish language in modern times, Ortega y Gasset,
is above all a literary figure.

Within this tradition, Borges' prose is an anom-
aly, for, in opting for the strictest frugality, he goes
against the Spanish language's natural tendency toward excess. To say that, with Borges, Spanish became "intelligent" may seem offensive to others who
write in that language, but it is not. What I am trying
to get at (in the wordy, roundabout way I have just
described) is that in Borges there is always a logical,
conceptual level to which all else is subservient. His
is a world of clear, pure, and at the same time unusual ideas that are expressed in a limpid, rigorous
prose crafted to highlight these ideas. "There is no
more elaborate pleasure than that of thought, and
we surrender ourselves to it," says the narrator of

"The Immortal" in words that give us a perfect picture of Borges. This story is an allegory of his fictional world; in it, intellectual concerns always devour and destroy the merely physical.

In developing a style of this kind, which so genuinely reflected his taste and background, Borges made a radical innovation in the stylistic tradition of Spanish. By purifying it, by intellectualizing and coloring it in such a personal way, he showed that the language about which—like his character Marta Pizarro—he was often so severe was potentially much richer and more flexible than tradition seemed to indicate. Provided that a writer of Borges' caliber attempted it, Spanish was capable of becoming as lucid and logical as French and as straightforward and nuanced as English. Like no other writer in our language, Borges teaches us that when it comes to literary Spanish, there is always more to be done, that nothing is final and permanent.

Yet, paradoxically, the most intellectual and abstract of our writers was at the same time a superb storyteller. One reads most of Borges' tales with the hypnotic interest usually reserved for reading detective fiction—a genre he cultivated by injecting it with metaphysics. But his attitude toward the novel was nothing short of scorn. Predictably, its realistic tendencies troubled him, because, with the exception of Henry James and a few other illustrious practitioners, the novel resists being bound to what is purely speculative and artistic. It is condemned to meld into the totality of human experience—not just ideas but also instinct, reality no less than fantasy, individuals as well as society. The novel's congenital imperfection—its grounding in human clay—was something that Borges found intolerable.

This is why, in 1941, he wrote in the foreword to *The Garden of Forking Paths* that "the habit of writing long books, of extending to five hundred pages an idea that can be perfectly stated in a few minutes, is a laborious and exhausting extravagance." This remark assumes that every book is an intellectual discourse, the expounding of a thesis. If that were true, the details of any work of fiction would be little more than superfluous garments hung on a handful of concepts, which could be isolated and extracted like a pearl from its shell. Can *Don Quixote, Moby-Dick, The Charterhouse of Parma, The Devils* be reduced to one or two philosophical ideas? Borges' statement is not useful as a definition of the novel, but it does reveal to us, eloquently, that the central concerns of his fiction are conjecture, speculation, theory, doctrine—and the dangers of sophism.

Owing to its brevity and compression, the short story is the genre most suited to the subjects that prompted Borges to write. Time, identity, dreams,

games, the nature of reality, the double, eternity—
thanks to his mastery of his craft—lost their vague-
ness and abstraction and became attractive, even dramatic. These preoccupations appear as stories that
usually start cleverly, with quite realistic, precise details and footnotes, often in a recognizable social context. Then at some point, imperceptibly or quite suddenly, they veer toward the fantastic or vanish into
philosophical or theological speculation. The facts
are never important or truly original in these tales,
but the theories that explain them and the interpretations they give rise to are. For Borges, as for his
ghostly character in "Utopia of a Tired Man," facts
"are mere points of departure for invention and reasoning." Reality and fantasy are fused through the
style and ease with which the narrator shifts from
one to the other, more often than not displaying dev-
astatingly sardonic erudition and an underlying skepticism that keeps in check any undue indulgence.

In a writer as sensitive, courteous, and—especially
after his growing blindness made him little more
than an invalid—frail as Borges was, the amount of
blood and violence in his stories is astonishing. But it
should not be. Writing is a compensatory activity,
and literature abounds with cases like his. Borges'
pages teem with knives, crimes, and scenes of tor-
ture, but the cruelty is kept at a distance by his fine

sense of irony and by the cold rationality of his prose, which never falls into sensationalism or pure emotion. This restraint lends a statuesque quality to the physical horror, giving it the nature of a work of art set in an unreal world.

Borges was always fascinated by hoodlums on the outskirts of Buenos Aires and knife fighters in rural Argentina. These hard-bitten men, with their sheer physicality, animal innocence, and unbridled instincts, were the exact opposite of himself. Yet he peopled a number of his stories with characters based on these myths and stereotypes, bestowing on them a certain Borgesian dignity—that is to say, an aesthetic and intellectual quality. The thugs, knife fighters, and cruel murderers of his invention are as literary—as unreal—as his characters of pure fantasy. They may wear ponchos or speak in a way that apes the language of the old-time gauchos from the interior, but none of this makes them any more realistic than the heresiarchs, magicians, immortals, and scholars from every corner of the globe who inhabit his stories. All have their origins not in life but in literature—they are, first and foremost, ideas magically made flesh, thanks to the craft of a great literary conjurer.

Each one of Borges' stories is an artistic jewel and some, like "Tlön, Uqbar, Orbis Tertius," "The Circular Ruins," "The Theologians," and "The Aleph," are masterpieces of the genre. The unexpectedness and subtlety of his themes are matched by an unerring sense of structure. Obsessively economical, Borges never includes a word or a piece of information that is superfluous, and details are sometimes left out to tax the reader's ingenuity. The exotic is an indispensable element of the magic he weaves, and this distancing adds to the allure. In a remark about one of his characters, Borges said, "The fellow . . . was an Arab; I made him into an Italian so that I could understand him more easily." But usually Borges did the opposite: the more removed in time or space his characters were from him or his readers, the better he could manipulate them, attributing marvelous qualities to them and making their often improbable experiences more convincing.

This is not to say that Borges' exoticism and local color have a kinship with the exoticism and local color of regionalist writers like Ricardo Güiraldes and Ciro Alegría. In their work the exoticism is spontaneous and stems from an excessively provincial, localized vision of the countryside and its customs, which the regionalist writer equates with the world. In Borges, the exoticism is a pretext. He uses it— with the approval or the ignorance of his reader— to slip rapidly, imperceptibly, out of the immediate world and into that state of unreality which, in common with the hero of "The Secret Miracle," Borges believes "is the prerequisite of art."

An inseparable complement to the exoticism in his stories is the erudition, the bits of specialized knowledge, usually literary but also philological, historical, philosophical, or theological, that approach but never overstep into pedantry. Borges freely flaunts his wide acquaintance with different cultures, but his learning, like his use of exotic settings and characters, appears in his stories to fulfill an exclusively literary function. It is a key element in his creative strategy, the aim of which is to imbue his stories with a certain color or atmosphere all their own. The erudition becomes a narrative device that he uses both decoratively and symbolically. In Borges' hands, theology, philosophy, linguistics, and so forth lose their original character and take on the quality of fiction, becoming part and parcel of a literary fantasy.

"I'm rotten with literature," Borges once confessed in an interview to Luis Harss, meaning that literature had taken over every corner of his mental life. As indeed it had taken over his fictional world— one of the most literary worlds any author has ever created. In it, the words, characters, and myths forged down through the years by other writers flock in and out, over and over, and so vividly that they somehow encroach on the objective world that is the usual context of any literary work. The reference point in Borges' fiction is literature itself. "Little has happened to me in my lifetime, but I have read much," Borges wrote teasingly in his afterword to "Dream-tigers." "Or, rather, little has happened more memorable than the philosophy of Schopenhauer or the verbal music of England."

This should not be taken literally, for any man's life, however uneventful, conceals more riches and mystery than the deepest poem or the most complex mental process. But the remark reveals a subtle truth about the nature of Borges' art, which, more than that of any other modern writer, comes of processing world literature and putting an individual stamp on it. His brief narratives are full of resonances and clues that extend to the furthest reaches of literary geography. This is no doubt why literary critics are tireless in their attempts to track down and identify Borges' endless sources. Arduous work it is, too, make no mistake, and what is more it is pointless, for what bestows greatness and originality to Borges' stories are not the materials he used but what he turned those materials into: a small imaginary world, populated by tigers and highly educated readers, full of violence and strange sects, acts of cowardice and uncompromising heroism, in which language and imagination replace objective reality, and the intellectual task of reasoning out fantasies outshines every other form of human activity.

This is a world of fantasy only in the sense that it contains supernatural beings and abnormal events, not in the sense that it is an irresponsible world, a game divorced from history and even from humankind. There is much that is playful in Borges, and on the fundamental questions of life and death, human destiny and the hereafter, he expresses more doubt than certainty. His world is not separated from everyday life experience or uprooted from the obligations of society. Borges' work is as grounded in the changing nature of existence—that common predicament of the human species—as any lasting literary work. How could it be otherwise? No work of fiction that turns its back on life or proves incapable of illuminating life has ever endured. What is singular about Borges is that in his world the existential and the historical, feelings and instincts, sex and psychology have been dissolved and reduced to an exclusively intellectual dimension. And life, that boiling chaotic turmoil, reaches the reader sublimated and conceptualized, transformed into literary myth through the filter of his prose—a filter of such perfect logic that it sometimes appears not to distill life to its essence but to suppress it altogether.

Poetry, the short story, and the essay are all complementary in Borges' work, and it is often difficult to fit a particular text into one genre rather than another. Some of his poems tell stories, and many of his short stories—the very brief ones especially— have the compactness and delicate structure of prose poems. But it is mostly between his essays and short stories that elements become switched, so that distinctions are blurred and the two genres fuse into a single entity. Something similar happens in Nabokov's novel *Pale Fire,* a work of fiction that has all the appearance of a critical edition of a poem. The critics hailed the book as a great achievement, and of course it is. But Borges had been up to the same sort of tricks for years—and with equal skill. Some of his more elaborate stories, like "The Approach to Al-Mu'tasim," "Pierre Menard, the Author of Don Quixote," and "An Investigation of the Works of Herbert Quain," purport to be book reviews or critical articles. In the majority of his stories, invention, the forging of a make-believe reality, follows a tortuous path, cloaking the tales in historical re-creation or in philosophical or theological inquiry.

Since Borges always knows what he is saying, the intellectual groundwork for this sleight of hand is quite solid, but exactly what is fictitious in his stories remains ambiguous. Lies masquerade as truths and vice versa—this is typical of Borges' world. The opposite may be said of many of his essays, such as "A History of Eternity" or the little pieces in his *Book of Imaginary Beings*. In them, amid the bits of basic knowledge upon which they rest, an added element of fantasy and unreality, or pure invention, filters through like magic and turns them into fiction.

No body of literary work, however rich and accomplished it may be, is without its dark side. In the case of Borges, his writing sometimes suffers from a certain cultural ethnocentricity. The black, the Indian, the primitive often appear in his stories as inferiors, wallowing in a state of barbarity apparently unconnected either to the accidents of history or to society but inherent in their race or cultural status. They represent a lower humanity shut off from what Borges considered the greatest of all human qualities: intellect and literary refinement. None of this is explicitly stated, and doubtless it was not even conscious; rather, it shows through in the slant of a certain sentence, or in his depiction of a particular form of behavior.

For Borges, as for T. S. Eliot, Giovanni Papini, and Pio Baroja, civilization could only be Western, urban, and almost—almost—white. The East survives, but only as an appendage—as it has come down to us through the filter of European translations of

Chinese, Persian, Japanese, or Arabic originals. The native Indian and African cultures that form part of Latin America are featured in Borges' world more as contrasts with the West's superiority than as varieties of a shared humanity. Perhaps this is because they were a small presence in the milieu where he lived most of his life. This myopia does not detract from Borges' many admirable qualities, but it is best not to sidestep this limitation when giving a comprehensive appraisal of his work. Certainly it offers further proof of his humanity, since, as has been said over and over again, no such thing as absolute perfection exists in this world—not even in the work of a creative artist like Borges, who comes as close as anyone to achieving it.

# 3

## ORTEGA Y GASSET AND
## THE REVIVAL OF A LIBERAL

Over a half century ago don José Ortega y Gasset died in Spain, and more than three-quarters of a century ago *The Revolt of the Masses*—perhaps his most widely read and translated work—was published. These two anniversaries should lead us to reconsider the ideas of one of the most elegant and intelligent liberal philosophers of the twentieth century. Various circumstances—the Spanish Civil War, the forty-year Franco dictatorship, and the rise of Marxist and revolutionary doctrines in Europe—caused him to be thought of as old-fashioned or, even worse, to be misconstrued as a conservative thinker. But as Friedrich Hayek demonstrated in his celebrated essay "Why I Am Not a Conservative," a chasm exists between liberalism and conservatism; Ortega y Gasset stood firmly on the liberal rim of that great gulf.

Although he never managed to systematize his philosophy into an organic body of ideas, in the innumerable essays, articles, lectures, and notes that comprise his vast oeuvre, Ortega y Gasset developed an unequivocally liberal discourse that was extraordinarily advanced for Spain at the time. He would have said it was radical (one of his favorite words)—as critical of the dogmatic extremism of the left as of the authoritarian, nationalist, and Catholic conservatism of the right. And many of his ideas are still relevant and topical today, as we witness the excessive economicism that intellectual liberals have confined themselves to in the wake of Marxism's bankruptcy.

This liberalism is best demonstrated in the book *The Revolt of the Masses.* Although first published in Spanish in 1930, it had been anticipated in articles and essays two or three years earlier. The book is structured around a brilliant perception: that the supremacy of elites has ended and that the masses, now liberated from their subordination, are having a decisive impact on everyday life, profoundly upsetting civil and cultural values and social conventions. Written just as communism and fascism were reaching new heights, in a period that witnessed not only union organization and nationalism but the rise of a popular culture of mass consumption, Ortega's intuition about the dangers of the "collective" precisely encapsulated one of the key features of modern life.

His criticism is based on a defense of the individual, whose sovereignty, according to Ortega, is being threatened—and in many ways has already been destroyed—by the unstoppable emergence of "the masses" in modern life. For Ortega, the concept of "the masses" in no way coincides with social class, and he specifically rejects the Marxist definition of the term. The masses to which Ortega refers embrace men and women of different social classes who have formed a collective entity by abdicating their individuality and becoming just a "part of the tribe." The masses, in Ortega's work, are a group of individuals who have become de-individualized, who have ceased to be free-thinking human units, and have dissolved instead into a collective that thinks and acts for them, more through conditioned reflexes—emotions, instincts, passions—than through reason.

During the years when he was writing his book, the masses were forming around Benito Mussolini in Italy, and in subsequent years they would group around Hitler in Germany, or Stalin ("the little father of the people") in Russia. According to Ortega, communism and fascism, are "two clear examples of substantial regression," of the transformation of the individual into the "mass-man." But in his definition of "massification," Ortega includes more than just the regimented multitudes that form around political bosses and absolute rulers in totalitarian regimes. The masses, for Ortega, are also a force in democracies, where the individual tends to become increasingly absorbed by various collectives that play leading roles in public life. In this phenomenon he sees, hidden beneath the garb of modernity, a return to primitivism and certain forms of barbarism. As a liberal thinker, he views the disappearance of the individual into the collective as a historical setback and a major threat to democratic civilization.

Published on the eve of the Second World War, the book also contains a surprising call for European unification. Ortega predicts that "Europe will be an ultra nation," melding the peoples of the old continent into a community without completely sacrificing their individual traditions and cultures. Ortega sees this union as the only possible salvation for a region that has lost the hegemony it enjoyed in the colonial period. Twentieth-century Europe, in his view, has fallen into decadence, while, around it, Russia and the United States seem bent on taking its former place. Ortega's audacious proposal in favor of a European union, which would actually begin to take shape half a century later, is one of the most prescient aspects of this work and an admirable example of the visionary insight he sometimes achieved.

*The Revolt of the Masses* also proposes another refined liberal principle: that part of Europe's decline is due to the unbridled growth of the state, whose suffocating, bureaucratic, interventionist net has "jugulated" the initiatives and creativity of citizens. As the masses have erupted into political and social life, one effect has been the cheapening and vulgarization of culture. Genuine artistic products are being replaced by caricatures or indistinguishable, mechanical versions, and an upsurge of bad taste, crudeness, and stupidity has been the inevitable result.

Ortega was a cultural elitist, but his elitism concerned the creation and quality of cultural goods, not their dissemination and consumption. With respect to the latter, his stance was universalist and democratic: culture and its products should be within everyone's reach. Ortega simply believed that great artists and intellectuals—those who introduced new models and new ways of understanding life and its artistic depiction—should set the aesthetic and intellectual standards of cultural life. He believed that if the aesthetic values and intellectual references for the whole of society were established by the average taste of the masses—of ordinary men and women— the result would be the brutal impoverishment of cultural life and nothing less than the suffocation of creativity. Ortega's cultural elitism is inseparable from his cosmopolitism, and from his conviction that true culture does not have regional and much less national borders but is universal. In this sense, his view is profoundly anti-nationalist.

In his defense of liberalism, Ortega insists that in a democratic society the state must be secular ("History is the reality of man. He has no other.") and that liberal ideology is profoundly incompatible with dogmatic Catholic thought, which he refers to as anti-modern. The future has not been predestined by an almighty deity, in his view. History is the work of humans only, and "everything is possible in history; triumphant, indefinite progress as well as periodic retrogression."

At the very least, the arguments and assertions in this book reveal a great independence of spirit and a strength of conviction that were capable of withstanding the intellectual and political pressures of his day. These were times, let us not forget, when the intellectual class was increasingly skeptical of democracy, which endured abuse equally from both the fascist right and the communist left. Ortega's contemporaries frequently gave in to the temptation to join one of these two extremes, with a marked preference for communism. But he was not among them.

Nevertheless, his liberalism, although genuine, is partial. His defense of the sovereign rights of the individual, of a small, secular state that stimulates rather than stifles individual liberty, of a plurality of opinions and criticisms, is not accompanied by a defense of economic freedom and the free market. Ortega approaches this aspect of social life with a mistrust resembling disdain, and occasionally he exposes surprising ignorance, especially for an intellectual with such curiosity about, and openness toward, most disciplines of thought. This disdain doubtless reflects, to some extent, the limitations of his generation. Without exception, like their Latin American counterparts, the Spanish liberals who were more or less Ortega's contemporaries, such as Ramón Pérez de Ayala and Gregorio Marañón (with whom he would form the Agrupación al Servicio de la República [Group in the Service of the Republic] in 1930), were liberals in a political, ethical, civic, and cultural sense but not in an economic sense. Their defense of civil society, democracy, and political liberty ignored a key part of liberal doctrine: that without economic freedom and the solid legal guarantee of private property and the enforcement of contracts, political democracy and public freedoms are vulnerable.

Although as a free thinker Ortega distances himself from the Catholic education he received in a Jesuit school and university, he shows traces of a Catholic moral system that mistrusts business, finance, economic success, and capitalism, as though these social activities reflect a base materialism which obstructs spiritual and intellectual growth. No doubt this is the source of his disparaging allusions to the United States, "the paradise of the masses," scattered throughout his book. With a certain cultural superiority, Ortega passes judgment on that country as having sacrificed its "qualities" for the quantities of a superficial culture. From that premise, he develops one of the few absurd notions in *The Revolt of the Masses:* that the United States will prove to be, by itself, incapable of the kind of scientific advancement that Europe has achieved. With the rise of the massman, Ortega believes, science is in danger of decline.

One consequence of the primacy of the massman in the life of nations, he says, is a loss of interest in the general principles of culture—an indifference, that is, to the very foundations of civilization. As the vulgar masses focus their attention on technology and the marvels it can produce, basic science—exploration of the natural world for its own sake—takes second place. Of course, without technology neither luxury automobiles nor painkillers would be possible, and Ortega is aware of that. But he compares Americans' deification of these consumer products with primitive African villagers' attraction to the seemingly magical trinkets of modern mass production.

Science can exist and prosper, says Ortega, only when it rests on the firm foundation of a long-established civilization. The United States, although powerful and productive, will never manage to surpass the purely technological phase of innovation it has reached: "Happy the man who believes that, were Europe to disappear, the North Americans could continue science!" This is a flawed prediction in a book full of prophecies that have become realities.

In *The Revolt of the Masses,* Ortega criticizes nationalism as typical of the growing power of the collective over the individual. He claims that the concept of nation-states built on communities defined by race, religion, or language is a myth. He inclines more toward Ernest Renan's idea of a nation as "a daily plebiscite," whose members reaffirm each day, with their behavior and adherence to laws and institutions, their desire to be "a unit of destiny." This idea of a nation whose citizenship is flexible and ever-changing, viewed alongside his prediction that Europe will soon become a supra-national union, seems like a utopian fantasy. And indeed, within a few years, belligerent nationalism would lead Europe to the carnage of the Second World War.

Ortega's *Epilogue for the English,* a critique of pacifism, was published in 1937, seven years after *The Revolt of the Masses* and at the height of the Spanish

Civil War. It criticizes the stereotypical view held by foreigners of what is actually happening within a society. Ortega presents as an example the case of English intellectuals who, "comfortably seated in their offices or their clubs," sign manifestos stating that the Spanish communists who coerce writers to sign manifestos or to speak on the radio in a way that serves their interests are "defenders of liberty." From all of this he concludes that foreign public opinion can be seen, in certain cases, as a "bellicose intervention" in the internal affairs of a country because of the lethal effects it may have on those affairs.

This leaky argument implies that the suppression of free speech and of the expression of political opinions by outsiders can be justified on the grounds of national security. Ortega fails to recognize that more is often known abroad about a dictatorship than in the country where it holds power, because internal censorship prevents those under the boot of totalitarianism from being fully aware of the situation in which they live.

But seen another way, this misguided statement reveals one source of the anxiety and despair Ortega experienced in the face of the Spanish Civil War. In his view, European intellectuals embellished the republic for ideological reasons, without taking into account the abuses and anti-democratic excesses that had been committed in its name. For this reason, Ortega could not or did not want to choose between the opposing parties during the civil war, especially since he had concluded that the conflict was not so much between democratic republicanism and fascism as between fascism and communism, an alternative Ortega equally rejected.

Nevertheless, Ortega's correspondence and the testimony of people close to him suggest that at one time he came to believe that Franco and the nationalists represented the lesser evil, although he never made this opinion public. It was a mistake for which he would be mercilessly reproached by posterity and which would contribute to isolating his work from so-called progressive intellectual circles. But in truth, as Ortega saw clearly, there is no lesser evil when choosing between two totalitarianisms—it is like choosing between two terminal diseases.

This is something that Ortega himself had the opportunity to confirm when he returned to Spain in 1945, at the end of the Second World War. He believed that the Allied victory over fascism would give him the opportunity to work toward the democratization of his country from the inside. In fact, he was never able to recover his university post or resume his public life. He could do little more than live in domestic exile, in a sort of limbo, under constant surveillance. Frustrated and anxious, he was forced to stand by while his work was misconstrued by the Falangists who wanted to make it their own. In his last ten years he lived an extremely unsettled life, making frequent trips between Spain and Portugal.

Reading Ortega y Gasset is always a joy, because of the beauty and eloquence of his style: clear, vivid, intelligent, cultured, sprinkled with irony and accessible to every reader. This very accessibility has caused some commentators to deny him the status of philosopher and refer to him only as a man of letters or a journalist. I would love for this to be true, because then philosophy would become superfluous, amply replaced by literature and journalism.

It is true that Ortega's prose can sound affected at times, as when he used the invented *rigoroso* instead of the standard *riguroso,* and when, in the two rules he established for intellectuals—to oppose and to seduce—his flirtatiousness and vanity led him to neglect the former obligation in favor of the latter. But these occasional weaknesses are more than offset by the vigor and grace he was able to inject into his ideas, which in his essays frequently seem like the living, unpredictable characters of Balzac's *La Comédie Humaine* that so enthralled him in his adolescence.

What helped to humanize Ortega's ideas was his

penchant for realism, which—in the great tradition of Spanish painting—was inseparable from his intellectual mission. In his view, neither philosophy in particular nor culture in general should be an exercise of rhetorical acrobatics enjoyed by a select few. The mission of culture is democratic: it should immerse itself in solving the problems of everyday life, and draw nourishment from exposure to those difficulties. Long before the French existentialists developed their thesis of the intellectual's "commitment" to his own time and society, Ortega had adopted this conviction and put it into practice in everything he wrote.

One of his celebrated phrases—"Clarity is the courtesy of the philosopher"—was a maxim he followed with dogged loyalty when he sat down to write. I do not believe that his effort to be accessible, inspired by Goethe's desire to move from obscurity to clarity (what he called the luciferian yearning), impoverished his thinking and reduced him to the role of a mere disseminator. To the contrary, one of his finest achievements was bringing the great issues of philosophy, history, and culture to a nonspecialist public—to common readers—in a way that enabled them to understand and feel concern about those issues, without trivializing or betraying them. This led him naturally to journalism and to public lectures, where he addressed vast, heterogeneous audiences, under the conviction that ideas confined to the classroom or to professional enclaves simply languished and died. He firmly believed that philosophy helps human beings figure out how to live, to resolve their difficulties, and to deal lucidly with the demands of their environment, and for this reason philosophical thought should not be the exclusive property of trained professionals but should be brought within the grasp of ordinary people.

Ortega y Gasset's obsessive drive to make all his readers understand his ideas is one of the great values he bequeathed to us. This demonstration of his democratic, liberal vocation is of utmost importance to us today, when jargon and other specialized, hermetic languages have replaced ordinary discourse. Often, such verbal gymnastics are mere trickery and obfuscation, rather than a necessary expression of complexity and scientific depth. Whether we agree or disagree with his ideas and arguments, one thing is evident about Ortega: he plays no tricks—the transparency of his prose does not allow it.

His luciferian yearning for clarity did not prevent him from making courageous observations and prescient predictions about the dominant trends of his age. As we have seen, in *The Revolt of the Masses* he warned with remarkable foresight that in the twentieth century, unlike earlier times, elites would no longer be the decisive factor in social and political evolution. They would be displaced by workers, peasants, the unemployed, soldiers, students, and collectives of all types, whose emergence in history—peaceful or violent—would revolutionize society and make a clear break with the past. In "The Dehumanization of Art" (an essay first published in Spanish in 1925), he described in meticulous and accurate detail the progressive divorce between modern art and the tastes and interests of the general public, a phenomenon without precedent in the history of civilization, driven by the formidable dominance of form that was introduced into music, painting, and literature by the avant-garde. These are but two examples of the lucidity with which Ortega scrutinized what he called his "circumstance" and perceived in it the dominant trends and power lines of the immediate future.

As a social critic, he demonstrated a surprising and felicitous intuition, but as a political theorist he did not fare as well. Free thinker, atheist (or at least agnostic), civilist, cosmopolitan, advocate of European union, democrat, and opponent of nationalism and all ideological dogmas, he advocated a "radical" analysis that struck at the root of social issues, never being content to languish on the surface. Nevertheless, in politics Ortega kept a relative distance from the radicalism he preached. His tolerance for a wide range of ideas and positions defined him as a liberal—but a liberal limited by his lack of economic knowledge. This void led him at times—as when he proposed solutions to problems such as centralism, despotism, or poverty—to call for an interventionist state and autocratic government totally at odds with the individual liberties and civil engagement he defended with such conviction and persuasive reasoning.

Ortega y Gasset put a lot of faith in the Spanish Republic, and its failures traumatized him. The Franco rebellion and the extremist polarization that led to the mayhem and bloodbath of civil war trapped him in a sort of ideological catacomb. In his view, liberal democracy was "the political model that has represented the highest form of coexistence," demonstrating a spirit of tolerance without historical precedent. Liberalism was "the right which the majority concedes to the minority"; it was "the decision to coexist with the enemy." But was such a position possible in the midst of a civil war? What he defended—an enlightened, European, civil, free society based on coexistence and the rule of law—seemed like a utopian impossibility in a Europe shaken by the advance of two totalitarian regimes which were crushing in their path the foundations of the civilization he had envisioned for Spain. Ortega never got over the collapse of those illusions.

When one reads the work of a writer for as long as I have read Ortega, albeit in small daily doses, one becomes so familiar with him—I mean with his person—that one has the sensation of having been on intimate terms with him, of having been present at one of those conversations with his friends, which, as Julián Marías and other disciples have described, were often brilliant. He must have been an extraordinary conversationalist, lecturer, and teacher. When reading his best essays, one *listens* to Ortega: his dramatic silences, the sibilant whip of the unusual adjective, and labyrinthine phrase that suddenly closes, rounding out an argument with the rhetorical flair of a bullfighter. Quite a show.

In recent times, Ortega has been much maligned by the left, which accuses him, as Gregorio Morán does in *El Maestro en el Erial: Ortega y Gasset y la Cultura del Franquismo* (1998), of having been a discreet accomplice of the nationalists during the civil war. Morán supports this claim with frail arguments—for example, that two of the philosopher's children fought with the rebels, or that he maintained friendships and correspondence with some Franco diplomats, or that he was eager to publish in

*The Times* of London, with the help of a representative of the nationalists in Great Britain, his text criticizing European intellectuals for having sided with the Republic without understanding Spanish reality. The alleged incident in which Ortega, with the intercession of a third party, offered to write Franco's speeches seems little more than a rumor. No reliable proof of this has ever surfaced, and his correspondence gives no hint of credence to the story. The truth is (and Morán's book more than demonstrates this) that if Ortega had wanted to be part of the Franco regime—a regime that both attacked and silenced him yet frequently attempted to bribe him—he would have been welcomed with open arms. He could have supported it publicly, with no need for discretion. He never did so.

Ortega continued to receive his university professor's salary at the time he retired, and this fact has also been used as an argument to discredit him. Of course, it would have been better if he had not done so. It also would have been better never to have returned to Spain in 1945 and to have died in exile instead, or to have firmly and unequivocally opposed the dictatorship. It would have been better because, if these things had happened, the confusion surrounding what he was, what he believed in and defended, would have been avoided, and it would have been easy to present him as a politically correct figure today.

But Ortega's true "circumstance" was not to take either side when the civil war broke out. The option of choosing had already been compromised by upheaval and political polarization during the Republic, which left him in a political no man's land. Despite this, and recognizing the vulnerability and isolation of his refusal to take sides, he remained true to his neutral position until his death. This was impractical in the context of such violent splits in his society and the belligerent Manichaeism expressed, in which nuance and moderation disappeared; but it was not dishonest. The civil, republican, democratic, plural regime he had defended in 1930, with the Group of Service to the Republic, was nothing like what was established in Spain after the fall of the monarchy. This led him to make a tormented admonition: "This is not it, this is not it!" But the alternative was not a fascist uprising either, which is why he abstained from publicly taking up the cause of either group and later from adhering to the regime that emerged victorious.

When Ortega returned to Spain in 1945, he did so convinced that the end of the war would bring about a transformation of the dictatorship. He was wrong, of course, and paid dearly for his mistake. He was vilified, on the one hand, by the ultraconservative sectors of the regime, who did not forgive his secular position. And on the other hand, he was forced to slip away like a cat from those who attempted to use him as a proto-ideologue of the Falange. These attempts reached grotesque proportions during the week of spiritual exercises undertaken by the School of Humanities of the University of Madrid for "the conversion of Ortega y Gasset," and the systematic campaigns organized from pulpits to persuade the philosopher to emulate his colleague, Manuel García Morente, who was touched by the Holy Spirit and returned to the Catholic fold.

Despite a timorous temperament that some critics reproached him for, Ortega resisted these immense pressures—which came not only from official bodies but also from people who respected him and whom he respected in turn—and he never wrote a single line to retract his ideas. This led the regime, on the eve of Ortega's death, to give the following order to the Spanish press, through Franco's Information Minister, Arias Salgado: "Faced with the possible contingency of the death of don José Ortega y Gasset . . . this newspaper will give the news with a headline of a maximum of two columns and the inclusion, if so desired, of a single eulogistic article, which will not omit his political and religious errors, and will not at any point use the term *maestro*."

Ortega's political mistakes were not those of a coward or an opportunist. At worst, they were the naive mistakes of a philosopher who was determined to offer a moderate, civil, and reformist alternative at a time when this option did not have the slightest possibility of flourishing in Spain. He should not be blamed for his tepidness, half-heartedness, and uncertainties. They demonstrate the dramatic destiny of an intellectual who was viscerally and rationally allergic to extremes, intolerance, absolute truths, nationalisms, and dogmas, be they religious or political. Of a thinker who for that very reason seemed anachronistic, a relic at a time when democratic coexistence was evaporating in the heat of a ferocious civil war, and later, during the totalitarian night. It was not only Ortega but also the democratic, liberal position that was traumatized by the slaughter of civil war.

But what about now? Are the ideas of Ortega y Gasset, which fascists and Marxists alike disdained, not in many ways a living, up-to-date reality in the plural, free, and resounding Spain of today? Instead of erasing him, modern history has endorsed Ortega as the most brilliant and coherent thinker that Spain has given to secular and democratic culture. He was also the one who wrote the best.

Contemporary liberal thought has much to learn from the ideas of Ortega y Gasset. Above all, to rediscover that—contrary to what those people bent on reducing liberalism to an economic recipe for free markets, fair play, low tariffs, controlled government spending, and the privatization of business, suppose—liberalism is, above all, an attitude toward life and society based on tolerance and coexistence, on respect for the rich history and unique experiences of different cultures, and on a firm defense of liberty. Liberalism recognizes that individual sovereignty is the driving force of material progress, of science, arts, and letters, and of a complex civilization in which the independence, rights, and responsibilities of individuals are held in balance with those of other individuals, protected by a system of laws guaranteeing the rights of minorities as well as the majority.

Economic freedom is a key element of the liberal doctrine, but certainly not the only one. We of course regret that many liberals of Ortega's generation were unaware of it. However, it is no less serious a mistake to reduce liberalism to an economic policy of free markets functioning with a minimum of government interference. Are not the numerous unsuccessful attempts to liberalize the economies of

Latin America, Africa, and Europe in recent decades clear proof that economic formulas can fail spectacularly if they are not supported by a body of ideas that makes them acceptable to the public? Liberal doctrine is a culture in the broadest sense of the word, and Ortega y Gasset's essays reflect this in a stimulating, cogent manner on every page.

If he had been French, Ortega would be as well known and widely read today as Sartre, whose existentialist philosophy of being "in situation" he anticipated—and presented in better prose. If he had been English, he would be another Bertrand Russell, at once a great thinker and a notable disseminator of his ideas. However, he was only a Spaniard, when the culture of Cervantes, Quevedo, and Góngora hovered in the basement (the image is his) of what were considered the great modern cultures. Today, things have changed and the doors of that exclusive club have opened to the vigorous language that he enriched and renewed as much as Jorge Luis Borges and Octavio Paz would do later. The moment has arrived for everyone to come to know José Ortega y Gasset and to give his thought and writing the recognition they deserve.

# 4

## THE CHALLENGE OF
## NATIONALISM

In *The Road to Serfdom* (1944–1945), Friedrich Hayek wrote that socialism and nationalism were the two greatest dangers facing civilization. The great Austrian economist surely would have amended that phrase today, replacing the term socialism with religious fundamentalism.

The socialism Hayek referred to was Marxist, the sworn enemy of liberal democracy, which it denigrated as a form of capitalist exploitation. That form of socialism aimed to end private ownership of the means of production, collectivize land, nationalize industry, centralize and plan the economy, and install the dictatorship of the proletariat as a first step toward a future classless society. Marxist socialism disappeared with the disintegration of the Soviet Union and the conversion of Communist China to single-party authoritarian capitalism. Its epitaph was the fall of the Berlin Wall in 1989.

Fortunately for democratic culture, the socialism that exists today, and enjoys excellent health, is socialist in name only. It accepts that private industry produces more employment and wealth than the public sector, especially in a market system, and it is an avid supporter of political pluralism, elections, freedom, and the rule of law. Socialism is no longer ideological; it has become ethical. Instead of preparing for revolution, it works to promote the welfare state and to enact public policies that ease the burdens of the unemployed, the elderly, the sick, and vulnerable minorities, as well as to redistribute wealth through taxation and to correct what it calls market imbalances.

In many cases, these economic and social policies are barely distinguishable from those advocated by liberals or conservatives. In fact, it would have been difficult in the late 1990s to identify significant differences between the economic policies of Britain's socialist government under Tony Blair and those of Spain's conservative (sorry, moderate) government under José María Aznar, or between those of Germany's Christian Democrat government under Helmut Kohl and those of the Social Democrat government under his successor, Gerhard Schröeder. This kind of

socialism is no longer an enemy but a key compo-
nent of democratic culture in the modern world.

By contrast with socialism, nationalism has not
adapted well to a changing world. Of course it is not
the same as it was when Hayek used the term, reflected in the terrible faces of Germany's Nazism, Italy's Fascism, or Spain's Francoism. Nationalism is
no longer as uniform or biased toward the extreme
right as it was then. Today it is an elusive, proliferate,
multiheaded beast that behaves in different, conflic-
ting ways. Many optimists believed, after the catastrophe of two world wars caused by nationalism,
that it would gradually fade away, or would remain
on the sidelines of Western political life, entrenched
in small groups with no electoral backing. And yet
what we have seen is a significant resurgence of nationalism in recent times.

This is especially true in Spain, where strong nationalist movements in Catalonia and the Basque
Country (and, to a lesser extent, in Galicia and the
Canary Islands) run the risk of fragmenting the very
sovereignty they challenge (some peacefully, others
through violent means). However, this is also true in
countries where nationalism once seemed less intense. For example, the Scottish National Party in
the United Kingdom was once a pleasant, quaint
movement with multicolored kilts and bagpipes. To-

day it is a major political force in Scotland, where, for the first time in the modern history of Great Britain, the polls indicate that almost half of all Scots are in favor of independence. In the 1990s, the National Front in France attracted between 15 and 20 percent of voters, and in Austria almost a third of voters backed the so-called Liberal Party of Jörg Haider. In Italy, the nationalist movement of Umberto Bossi, the Lombard League, was intent on tearing the country apart, separating the entire north—the ethereal Padania—from the rest of the country.

It could be argued that, with these few brief examples of nationalist movements, I am putting too many different eggs—hen, quail, ostrich, and even the literary basilisk eggs—in the same basket. Are these movements all the same thing? One of the major difficulties in discussing nationalism is precisely that it is a polymorphic doctrine which reproduces and manifests itself in different forms. Yet, at its secret core, this diversity includes several common features that I will try to describe, because it is this essence, not the outer shell, that poses a challenge to democratic culture.

A leader of the Mexican Institutional Revolutionary Party (PRI) is said to have explained the ideological affiliation of his party with this statement, worthy of the celebrated Mexican comedian Mario

Moreno's character Cantinflas: "The PRI is not of the right or of the left but just the opposite." Such conceptual gibberish emerges when attempts are made to place nationalism within the traditional categories of left and right. It moves without difficulty between these poles, sometimes adopting a radical face, such as the Basque separatist organization ETA, the Catalan Terra Lliure, or the Irish Republican Army (IRA) in Northern Ireland, and sometimes identifying with unequivocally conservative positions, such as Convergència i Unió or the Basque Nationalist Party (PNV). Often, nationalisms are left-wing during their rebellious phase, only to become right wing when they attain power, as was the case of the Algerian National Liberation Front (FLN) and almost all Arab nationalist movements.

I am keenly aware of the great divide that separates nationalists who practice terrorism from those who act within the law and reject violent tactics. Defending an ideal peacefully, through elections and within the legal system, can help to facilitate social coexistence, whereas killing, kidnapping, and car bombing can inflame a situation until it explodes in an orgy of blood, as happened in Bosnia and Kosovo. But without in any way undervaluing movements that are committed to the rule of law, I must say that it is not the method that determines whether or not a political movement is nationalist but rather the basic set of tenets and beliefs to which all nationalists—whether peaceful or violent—subscribe.

I have deliberately said tenets and beliefs, not ideas. All nationalist doctrine is based on an act of faith, not on a rational, empirical conception of history and society. Nationalism is a *collectivist* act of faith that imbues a mythical entity—the nation—with a fictive coherence, homogeneity, and unity preserved over time, untouched by historical change. Along with this sense of a timeless community, nationalism demands a belief in metaphysical essentialism—the doctrine that individuals do not exist separately from the national womb that gave them their being and identity (a crucial term of nationalist rhetoric). The social, cultural, and political birthright of the nation is manifested in the language its people speak, the way they behave, the history they share, the land they claim, and often the common religion, ethnicity, or race—even the cranial shape and blood type—which God or chance has bestowed upon them.

This utopian notion of a perfectly homogeneous, unified community disappears as soon as we try to apply it to concrete nations in the real world. To differing degrees, all of them are culturally, racially, and socially heterogeneous, so the notion of a collective identity—not to mention a national identity—is a fallacious concept that ignores the rich diversity of humankind. Nationalism gets around such contradictions by playing another card, victimization—it serves up a long list of historical grievances to demonstrate the ways in which colonizing powers have tried to destroy or contaminate the victim nation. But however much the colonizers might try (according to this view), they will not succeed: the nation will survive, regardless of the brutality of the crimes committed by the conqueror, or the centuries of systematic genocide, or the frequency of invasions, occupations, and dispossessions. The victim nation may be forced to feign "acculturation" for a time; but underneath, it continues to resist, preserving its essence, remaining true to its origins, holding its soul intact, awaiting the hour when its sovereignty and liberty will be redeemed.

Of course, this list of offenses by strong nations against weak ones has some basis in historical truth. It would be a mistake, however, to believe that violence and abuse explain the emergence of nationalism. If this were true, nationalism would spread like an epidemic across all regions of the planet. Is there any place that has not suffered some historical injustice? There is no society that has not, at one time or another, faced a horrific spectacle of unspeakable crimes and violations committed both horizontally (between societies, peoples, and nations) and vertically (between powerful groups and individuals against defenseless groups and individuals within each society). The history of all countries is, in part, a tragic tale of infamy. Does anyone doubt that the people of Extremadura, Andalusia, or Castile have suffered less from the domination, intolerance, and abuses of the powerful than the Basques, Catalans, or Galicians? It is only when viewed through the lens of nationalism that these historical injustices become collective and hereditary, like original sin.

Nationalism needs those historical offenses to justify its claims of communal victimization and atavistic injustice, which only the regaining of lost independence (and often the reconquest of lost land) will rectify. It also needs these offenses to explain the supposed adulteration of national unity with respect to language, culture, institutions, and even race, and to justify policies that seek to re-establish the purity and integrity of a nation tainted by decades or centuries of foreign domination.

Catalonia is a bilingual society that has roughly 50 percent Catalan speakers and 50 percent Spanish speakers, though almost all Catalan speakers also speak Spanish. The bilingualism of Catalan speakers is, in truth, a privilege that makes most of them lords and citizens of two cultures and traditions to which they belong equally, because, as Vidal-Quadras has pointed out, in Catalonia "the two languages are not separated by a dividing frontier; both are present in each province, in each region, in each city, in each neighborhood, in each building, in each landing."

But to accept this cultural reality would put the Catalan nationalists in a tight spot, since it would force them to revise their basic assumption of linguistic homogeneity and cultural unity and to design education and cultural policies that respect and foster bilingualism. Since no individual is likely to rethink his own position, much less a political party, the nationalists in power continue to claim that the cultural situation in Catalonia is the result of historical abuse—of persecution to which the Catalan language and culture have been subjected by governments that imposed the dictates of the imperial power. The policy of "linguistic normalization" is designed, then, to remedy that past injustice by imposing Catalan as the preferred (and sometimes only) language taught in schools and used in the administration. In practice, however, this correction has become an equivalent injustice—discrimination against Spanish speakers.

Such policies are inevitable whenever nationalist parties are true to themselves—that is, when they try to convert the fiction of nationality into reality. Due to its own dynamics, nationalism's policy of "positive discrimination" or "normalization" (lovely euphemisms) sometimes goes beyond the benign, reasonable limits within which the authorities attempt to contain it. In truth, measures designed to shift the current reality of a bicultural or multicultural society back to a mythical linguistic unity eventually lead to human rights violations, beginning with the rights of individuals to liberty and free choice.

Many Basque nationalists, well-intentioned pacifists, were undoubtedly horrified when it came to light that in an *ikastolak* school of the Basque Country, all children caught speaking Spanish instead of Basque were forced to fill their pockets with stones as punishment. These Basques were sincere in saying that the excess zeal of some militants or isolated officials did not represent the policy of the regional government. Nevertheless, the truth is that in the conception of humankind, society, and history endorsed by the ideology of nationalism, there is a seed of violence that inevitably germinates whenever nationalists try to meet the demands of their own postulates, especially the main one: to rebuild what Benedict Anderson calls the "imagined community," an illusory nation that is culturally, socially, and linguistically integrated and whose human offspring gain their identity from membership in this collective.

In the case of ETA, the Basque intellectual Fernando Savater explains the irrevocable link between totalitarianism and nationalism in the following way: "Totalitarianism is not merely showing hostility to a political rival, it is the systematic denial, extermination, of other points of view. For ETA, the only viable Basques—in other words, those who are not candidates for exile or assassination—are nationalists of one stripe or another, regardless of whether they were the ones who mistakenly accepted the Statutes of Autonomy, the heroes that rejected it from the beginning or the converts who eventually saw the light. The rest are recently emboldened Spanish patriots living among the Basques, who are openly accused of 'social persecution' and with whose parties any type of political agreement is resolutely prohibited, *exeunt omnes*."

Because real history does not fit the nationalists' version of the past, or does so only awkwardly, nationalism inevitably embellishes or distorts it, to serve its purposes and establish its foundations. A book that is essential reading—*El Bucle Melancólico* by Jon Juaristi—documents with a wealth of information and great analytical subtlety this process of fictionalizing the history of Basque nationalism to bring it politically up to date. Most of the poems, songs, stories, articles, and memoirs that Juaristi examines have specific local interest but little literary value (the Unamuno essays are one of the exceptions), though little literary value. Nevertheless, despite the artistic and conceptual poverty of those texts, they contain certain sentimental, religious, and ideological themes that shed light on the reason for the existence of nationalism in general and of ETA terrorism in particular.

Juaristi defines melancholy as the longing for what did not exist, a state of ferocious nostalgia for something wonderful that is gone, something that combines happiness with justice, beauty with truth, health with harmony: a paradise lost. The fact that this nation was never a tangible reality is no obstacle for people who, blessed with the terrible, formidable instrument that is the imagination, manage to fabricate it. This is why fiction exists: to populate the emptiness of life with phantoms that human beings require in order to make sense of their own cowardice, generosity, fear, pain, or stupidity. The ghosts that fiction inserts into reality can be benign, innocuous, or malignant. Nationalism's specters fall into this last group.

Juaristi describes the process of building myths, rituals, liturgies, fantasies, legends, and linguistic ravings that seal Basque nationalism in a solipsist vacuum, preserving the fiction and isolating it from critical examination. The truths that nationalist ideology proclaims are not rational: they are dogmas. And like churches, nationalist groups do not engage in true dialogue: they sanctify and excommunicate. Nationalism feeds on instinct and passion, not intelligence; its strengths lie not in ideas but in beliefs and myths. For this reason, it is closer to literature and religion than to philosophy or political science, and to understand it, poems, novels, and rhetoric can be more useful than historical and sociological studies. Benedict Anderson, in *Imagined Communities,* shows through the fiction of the Filipino José Rizal, the Mexican José Fernández de Lizardi, and the Indonesian Mas Marco Kartodikromo where the idea of a nation in these former European colonies was born.

That nationalist ideology is essentially unfettered by objective reality and is forced to distort history systematically to justify itself does not mean, of course, that the grievances, injustices, and frustrations within a given society do not serve to fan the flames of rebellion. Nevertheless, reading *El Bucle Melancólico,* one notes something alarming: even if the Basque country had not been subjected, especially during the Franco regime, to humiliation and intolerable restrictions on the use of the Basque language and local traditions, the nationalist seed would have germinated anyway because the soil on which it falls and the fertilizers that make it grow are not of this world. They exist, as in novels and legends, in our innermost subjectivity. They appear as a response to our dissatisfaction with and rejection of existing reality, and they are channeled by certain minorities—nationalist parties—in order to achieve political power.

What Juaristi, with Freud's help, called melancholy—the first impulse that feeds nationalism—Karl Popper defined as the "temptation of the tribe," or the reluctance of human beings to take on the obligations and risks of individual liberty, seeking protection instead in some collective entity, in this case the nation (in other cases race, class, or religion). For Emile Durkheim, collectivist ideologies such as nationalism arose as a result of the disappearance of traditional hierarchies and social orders due to the centralization and bureaucratic rationalization that industrial progress required. Seeing themselves deprived of the emotional and social security of these pre-industrialized societies, human beings sought refuge in collectivism. National belonging—the privilege of being part of a select and exclusive dynasty, ontologically unified, of dead, living, and future beings—was transformed into a supreme value.

For Elie Kedourie, one of the most perceptive analysts of this ideology, nationalism was born as a doctrine derived from the Kantian theory of the self-determination of individuals. As Kedourie points out, Fichte replaced Kant's idea with the theory of the self-determination of nations, which gave back to individuals the identity they had lost. Without intending to do so, the German theologian Johann Gottfried von Herder completed this idea with his fervent defense of cultures and languages as the foundations of a nation. For Kedourie, this is the path nationalist doctrines followed to establish their place in modern history. In some cases these doctrines became radicalized with racist concepts and messianic ravings, which reached apocalyptic proportions with Hitler.

This path was not the only route to nationalism, however. In the developing world it began as a response to colonialism and the imperialist policies of Western powers. Examples include both Zionism and Arab nationalist movements. According to Ernest Gellner, nationalism gives birth to nations, rather than the other way around. He says that nationalism, a typical product of industrial society, selectively uses a country's pre-existing proliferation of cultures and transforms them in a radical and ingenious way, reviving dead languages, inventing traditions, and restoring fictive purities.

Given the diverse nature of nationalist movements, we should be cautious about generalizations, but one assertion that can be made without hesitation is that nationalism has an irrational core. Whether it is born of melancholy, desperation, anomie, fear of freedom, or protest against colonial invasion, this irrationality at its heart causes nationalism to drift easily into violence. At times, it leads groups to commit abominable crimes in the name of their ideal, such as has happened in Spain and Northern Ireland. Although moderate, pacifist nationalists and activists of irreproachable democratic credentials do exist, this does not alter the undeniable fact that a coherent nationalism, pushed to its logical conclusion, eventually leads to intolerant, discriminatory practices and open or veiled racism. There is no escaping it. Since the homogeneous nation of cultural, ethnic, and sometimes religious purity that it attempts to restore never in fact existed—or if it did exist, it disappeared over the course of history—nationalism is obliged to create this nation anew, to impose its own reality on a diverse society, and the only way to do so is through force.

The ravages of nationalism are probably more evident in language, literature, and art than in any other area of social life. If belonging to that collective abstraction, the nation, is the supreme value, and if this is the prism through which literary and artistic creations are judged, what can one expect to emerge from such a confusing and absurd set of premises? A nationalist perspective has little tolerance for works of art that are universal or cosmopolitan, that do not offer an explicit regional, national, or folkloric content. For nationalism, the most respected and respectable artistic creations are those that confirm its penchant for a collective identity. In practice, this leads to a kind of provincial self-absorption. This is why nationalism has not produced anything memorable in literature and the arts and why, as Ernest Gellner points out, "the prophets of nationalism were not anywhere near the First Division, when it came to the business of thinking."

To illustrate my point, I would like to quote another recent book, *Contra Catalunya,* by Arcadi Espada. The author, a Catalan journalist, bases his account on his experiences as a young man who suffered the final years of Francoism and witnessed the transition to freedom. He describes how, in the migration from a fascist dictatorship to democracy, Catalonia became impoverished by a nationalism that has dominated the region's political and cultural life for several decades. His book undermines nationalism not by making ideological arguments but by revealing the intolerable ravings and schmaltz it produces, as well as its slow suffocation of critical thought.

Out of fear of being accused of acting "against Catalonia," which is a kind of moral demonization, few dare to contradict certain myths and taboos imposed by the nationalists. Those who have the courage to do so, like Aleix Vidal-Quadras, know what to expect. Espada says that thanks to this invisible censorship, many topics have become untouchable or distorted to such an extent that they have become unrecognizable. These range from not mentioning the fascist position that many Catalans adopted during the Civil War and the Franco dictatorship, to the magical elimination of the social and economic importance of the region's many immigrants. These immigrants do not speak Catalan but they are nevertheless Catalans since they live and work there and have contributed with their labor, over two or more generations, to Catalonia's prosperity.

The men and women of this vast sector—Espada calls them "the poor"—are not represented in the Generalitat nationalist government; they have been gradually reduced to a ghost-like status, to cultural pariahs. They have been marginalized by an idea of Catalonia that forces stark simplifications on them: are you an insider or an outcast? With numerous examples, Arcadi Espada's book demonstrates the provincialism and foolishness to which a nationalist cultural policy, which looks to promote "identity," is doomed. In Espada's testimony—and in some polemical newspaper articles by Féliz de Azúa and the political essays of Aleix Vidal-Quadras—one sees the damage that nationalism has inflicted on a land long known as the most cultured and European region of Spain. Catalonia has regressed culturally, thanks to a doctrine that insists on putting signs up everywhere that read: "For Catalans only." But not even for all Catalans—only those that match the nationalist identikit.

I am neither a private pessimist nor a professional optimist. I believe that one's intellectual—but not artistic—duty is to try to remain within the bounds of realism. And realism demands recognizing that nationalism—or nationalisms, if one prefers—is the most serious problem facing Spain, a problem which, no doubt, has been considerably alleviated but not resolved with ETA's decision to lay down arms and negotiate a truce. This has understandably raised high hopes in Spain, and especially in the long-suffering Basque community. However, it would be naive, not to say blind, to suppose that this recent peace guarantees a quick, definitive solution to the problem of nationalisms in Spain. Concessions and political and ideological agreements generally inflame rather than pacify nationalism. They are like a red flag to a bull, causing it to make ever more demands.

The 1978 Spanish Constitution is an admirable ethical and legal attempt to make Spain a pluralistic, democratic society, "a nation of nations and regions," in the words of Gregorio Peres-Barba, one of the constitutionalists. The Constitution and the Statutes of Autonomy recognized the right of Catalonia, the Basque Country, and Galicia to consider themselves "nations," a category that is higher than and distinct from the category "regions," and to develop and promote their language and culture in complete freedom. In addition, it granted them broad administrative, economic, educational, and political authority. Many believed that the Statutes of Autonomy would serve to prevent the powder keg of nationalist recriminations against the central government from exploding. They hoped that broader sectors of Catalonia, the Basque Country, and Galicia would come around to this idea of coexistence within the diversity of a decentralized, pluralistic Spain as established in the Constitution.

Twenty years later, it was clear that this hope was an illusion. Instead of withering, nationalist movements became more robust, and they continue to make accusations of injustice, marginalization, prejudice, and discrimination against the Spanish state, which they view as something foreign and even hostile. The leader of the PNV, Arzalluz, said as much with stunning clarity: "The Basque Country does not fit in this Constitution." It is as if, from the perspectives of Catalonia, the Basque Country, and Galicia, the 1978 Constitution and the Statutes of Autonomy signified little more than a change of disguises, underneath which democratic Spain, just like dictatorial Spain, would continue oppressing its internal "colonies." This is a delirious ideological fantasy, but when an electoral majority supports a falsehood, as occurred in Catalonia and the Basque Country, or when a large number of voters back it, as in Galicia, it becomes a disturbing political reality.

The fact that elections forced the Spanish Socialist Workers Party (PSOE) and then the Popular Party (PP) to join forces with nationalist parties to be able to form a government awakened hope in some. They imagined that this alliance would help to mitigate the ultimate goal of nationalism—independence—and that the assumption of responsibilities in the central government would increasingly dilute the nationalists' aims until they became compatible, first in practice, then in theory, with the idea of a pluralistic Spain. Unfortunately, this did not occur either. The Convergència i Unió, and Basque Nationalist parties gave support to the government party to ensure its survival, but they did not co-govern with it. Instead, they used their privileged position to pressure the central government, demand concessions, and advance their own agenda, which did not shift even a fraction of an inch from its original form.

Of course, all of this is perfectly legitimate; it is the way democracy works. Clearly, however, the circumstantial parliamentary alliance of peripheral nationalisms with the so-called statist parties (a dreadful term) has not served to modify one jot the political conviction of those who, within the law and without the sound and fury of the extremists, work systematically to achieve their final objective, sugarcoated with a delicate rhetorical wrapping: self-determination. In plain English, this means the disintegration of Spain.

I do not believe that this disintegration will take place, nor do I want it to occur, obviously. It is not because I am a "Spanish nationalist" or anything of the sort, but because I am convinced that the splintering of Spain into a handful of independent nations (how many—three? four?) would not bring Basques or Catalans more freedom, or better living conditions, or a richer cultural life, or more opportunities for development or work. Instead, it would lead to widespread impoverishment in all of these areas, along with social unrest and government responses of a very uncertain (and perhaps sinister) nature. Although the dissolution of Czechoslovakia did not mean the end of the world for the Slovaks who demanded it, it did lead to an increasingly mediocre society governed by a corrupt, authoritarian pseudo-democracy headed by the nationalist Vladimir Meciar. In Serbia, Croatia, and Bosnia, the explosion of nationalism that destroyed Yugoslavia led to more than 200,000 deaths and bathed Kosovo in blood.

Other than satisfying the desire for power of certain political groups, achieving the nationalist ideal would mean a setback rather than progress for the democratic culture of Catalonia, the Basque Country, and Galicia. In these regions, even when nationalists obtain a majority in terms of votes, vast sectors of the population—majorities, in absolute terms—have not succumbed to the propaganda and rhetoric of the nationalist fiction, despite whatever solidarity and loyalty they may feel for their small, unique world. In addition to identifying themselves as Catalans, Basques, or Galicians, these people also feel Spanish and want to continue to be part of Spain, the ancient country, the shared multiracial, multicultural homeland whose vicissitudes, hopes, defeats, and comebacks they view as their own, which in fact they are. These populations want to continue to be Spanish and to participate with a discrete voice in the debate on nationalism—a strange debate in which the leading voice is almost exclusively that of the nationalists.

Some brave minorities fight it, of course, without letting themselves be intimidated. But many of them do not make their arguments against nationalism heard because the political situation forces them to be prudent. In Basque Country, until very recently, they risked their lives if they did so. Or they remain silent because they have already been defeated by the nationalists' moral intimidation, which has effectively turned those who criticize peripheral nationalisms into reactionary "Spanish nationalists." Of course, this is another fiction. As moral blackmail, however, it has managed to silence many Basques and Catalans. The only people in Spain today who can legitimately be called "Spanish nationalists" are insignificant groups and factions posturing on the extreme right, without voter support.

The truth is that typical Spaniards observe these nationalisms with a mixture of apathy and fatalism, as if the issue did not concern them, or as if their intervention would be pointless, because whatever has happened was destined to occur. This skeptical attitude can be highly civilized; it can also be suicidal. No one has expressed this warning better than the Catalan philosopher Eugenio Trías: "Before the understandable reaction of annoyance and irritation to the harassment of peripheral nationalisms, it would be lethal if an increasingly perceptible attitude among many Spaniards were to spread: 'Go away and leave us alone; if they do not establish borders and customs offices, we will establish them ourselves.' This attitude has a demoralizing effect on sectors that suffer nationalist excesses not by remote control but within the communities where they are dominant."

My opinion is that nationalists should be intellectually and politically challenged, all of them, head on, without apology, and not in the name of a different type of nationalism (the nonsense of "Spanish nationalism") but on behalf of democratic culture and freedom—that is, in the name of the culture that the vast majority of Spaniards embraced with enthusiasm in 1978, and whose spirit permeates the current Constitution and Statutes of Autonomy. This "project suggestive of shared life," according to Ortega y Gasset's formula, or "daily plebiscite," in the words of Ernest Renan, stretches Spanish decentralization to the limit to guarantee cultures, traditions, and regional peculiarities on the one hand and preserve national unity on the other. These texts can be amended and improved upon, of course—reform is a driving force of progress—without betraying the pluralistic spirit that inspires them.

This balance between local traditions and national unity is not fundamental just to Spain's future as it faces the formidable challenge of playing a leading role in the Europe Union. Above all this balance is necessary so that Spanish society can develop in a free, diverse, and rational manner a set of concepts that are profoundly alien to nationalist ideologies and practices. Nationalism will only begin to relinquish the field when the regions where it is currently encamped realize what is, for those of us who fight nationalism, a transparent truth: that there is no real grievance, injustice, prejudice, or marginalization on the nationalist agenda that cannot be remedied or resolved within the system of liberties and laws prevailing in Spain today, and that, to the contrary, this regime of pluralism and freedom will be seriously compromised if the exclusivist, discriminatory plans of nationalism triumph.

If this truth were accepted by a significant majority in the peripheral regions of Spain—and that is not an impossible dream—then nationalism would perhaps undergo a transformation like the one that turned socialism into a democratic force in modern times: emptying its contents and changing its nature, while keeping the name and some of the rhetoric. Nationalism might abandon its collectivist, exclusive attitude and perhaps adopt a line in defense of cultural diversity, which is, incidentally, in the tradition of nationalism's most respectable early critic, Johann Gottfried von Herder, to whom the term *nationalis-*

*mus* is attributed. He is no doubt the only thinker of intellectual weight of which nationalist ideology can boast. But Herder was not a nationalist in the political and statist sense that would gain currency after his death. As one of the harshest critics of the philosophy of the Enlightenment, he had the same distrust of the state that we modern-day liberals have. The nation that he defended with so much spirit and erudition was not a political entity but a cultural reality.

Rather than the father of nationalism, Herder should be considered the father of contemporary cultural diversity. Like many of his German compatriots, he celebrated the French Revolution at first, but the Jacobin Terror and the conquests of the revolutionary army transformed him into a sworn enemy of everything that tended to standardize or dissolve local cultures with a universal formula. He defended the exception, the particular, the right of smaller languages and traditions to survive, to not be crushed and erased by larger ones—not only a perfectly valid position from the perspective of democracy but a basic requirement for its existence. Herder was the first thinker to see, before the word and concept existed, the threat that what we now call "globalization" poses for local diversity. He clearly opposed the sacrifice of concrete, private individuals in the name of political generalizations.

If confined to the limits set by Herder, nationalism could provide a valuable service to democratic culture. But let us not fool ourselves: it will only restrict itself to those limits when an intellectual and political offensive, and a sufficiently persuasive electorate, leave it no alternative.

The Chilean historian Claudio Véliz tells us that when the Spaniards arrived, the Araucanian Indians had a belief system that contained no concepts for aging and natural death. For them, man was young and immortal. Physical decline and death could only be the work of magic, the evil arts, or enemy weapons. Undoubtedly, this conviction, both simple and convenient, helped the Araucanian Indians become the ferocious warriors they were. However, it did not help them develop an original civilization.

The Araucanian attitude is far from unusual. In fact, it is a widespread phenomenon. To attribute the cause of our misfortunes or defects to someone else—to others—is a stratagem that has allowed innumerable societies and individuals, if not to escape their misfortunes, at least to withstand them and live with a clear conscience. Masked behind subtle reasoning, hidden beneath lush rhetoric, this attitude is the root, the secret foundation, of cultural nationalism, which in the twentieth century, despite two world wars, has grown in intensity.

Cultural nationalism considers the indigenous as

an absolute, unquestionable value, and views anything foreign with disdain, as something that undermines, impoverishes, or weakens the spiritual nature
or essence of a country. This thesis can hardly stand
up to even superficial analysis, and it is easy to demonstrate how biased and naive its arguments are, as
well as the unreality of its central aim—cultural au-
tarchy. Nevertheless, history shows us that cultural
nationalism easily takes root and that not even countries with ancient, solid civilizations are immune to
it. To take some obvious examples, Hitler's Germany,
Mussolini's Italy, Stalin's Soviet Union, Franco's
Spain, and Mao's China all practiced nationalism in
an attempt to create an uncontaminated culture,
shielded through dogma and censorship from loath-
some corrupting agents—from foreignness and cosmopolitanism. In the last decades of the twentieth
century, it was in the smaller developing countries of
the Third World that cultural nationalism was most
vehemently preached, and where it found the most
followers.

Nationalism's defenders start with a false assumption: that the culture of a country is, like the natural
riches and raw materials harbored in its soil, something that should be protected from the voracious
avarice of imperialism, and kept stable, intact, un-
adulterated, and undefiled. To fight for "cultural in-

dependence," or to become emancipated from "foreign cultural dependence" in an attempt to "develop our own culture," are the standard formulas voiced by the so-called progressives of the Third World. That these pet phrases are hollow gibberish does not prevent them from seducing many people with their whiff of patriotism. (And in the realm of patriotism, Borges wrote, people only tolerate certainties.) They even persuade groups thought to be invulnerable to the authoritarian ideologies that these phrases disguise. People who claim to believe in political pluralism and economic liberty, to be hostile to single truths and omnipotent, omniscient states, frequently subscribe to nationalist sentiments without questioning what they mean. And the reason is very simple: nationalism is the culture of the uncultured.

Latin Americans in particular must directly challenge notions of cultural nationalism because this dogma is a major obstacle to our own cultural development. If these narrow beliefs, which have been validated by ignorance on the one hand and demagogy on the other, are allowed to prosper, we in Latin America will never have a rich, creative, modern spiritual life that expresses us in all our diversity and reveals us to ourselves and to other peoples of the world. If the proponents of cultural nationalism win the match and their theories become the official policy of the state—that "philanthropic ogre," as Octavio Paz called it—the result will be our intellectual and scientific stagnation and artistic suffocation. We will remain cultural adolescents—or worse, a picturesque anachronism, a folkloric exception, patronized by civilized communities to satisfy their desire for exoticism and their nostalgia for a barbarian age.

Truly "dependent" and "emancipated" cultures do not actually exist in the real world. There are poor cultures and rich ones, archaic and modern, weak and powerful. But we are all unavoidably interdependent. This has always been true, and even more so nowadays, since the extraordinary advance of communications has broken down the barriers between nations and made all peoples immediate, simultaneous co-participants in the present. No culture has originated, developed, and reached its prime without both feeding on and nourishing other cultures, in a continuous process of give and take, reciprocal influence, and miscegenation. The notions of "indigenous" and "alien" cultures are dubious, not to say absurd, and it would be extremely difficult to determine what corresponds to each one. In the only area where these terms have meaning—that of language—it is nevertheless impossible to align linguistic groups with the specific geographic and political borders of a country or to use those groups as a way to set a boundary for cultural nationalism.

To take a simple example, is the Spanish Peruvians speak, together with some 300 million other people around the world, "native" or "foreign" for us? And who among the Quechua speakers of Peru, Bolivia, and Ecuador are the legitimate owners of the Quechua language and tradition and who are the "colonized" and the "dependent" that should seek emancipation from them? This kind of question is as baffling as asking which national literature has a patent on the interior monologue, that key resource of modern narrative. Is it France, because of Édouard Dujardin, the mediocre novelist who was apparently the first to appropriate it? Or Ireland, because of the celebrated monologue of Molly Bloom in James Joyce's *Ulysses,* which made it revered in literary circles? Or the United States, where, thanks to the wizardry of William Faulkner, the interior monologue acquired unimagined flexibility and sumptuousness? In the realm of culture, including language and literature, the path of nationalism eventually leads to confusion and absurdity. What is certain is that indigenous and foreign cultural influences are indistinguishable, and originality is not at odds with these many influences or even at odds with imitation and adaptation. Culture can flourish only if it is closely interdependent with other cultures. Those who try to impede this process will not save "national culture," they will kill it.

In the field with which I am most familiar, it is not difficult to demonstrate that Latin American writers who gave our literature a more personal stamp were, in every case, those who exhibited fewer "inferiority complexes" when faced with foreign cultural values and who fully and unabashedly exploited them at the moment of creation. If modern Latin American poetry has a birth certificate, it is *modernismo,* and the father is Rubén Darío. Is it possible to conceive of a poet more "dependent," more "colonized" by foreign models than that universal Nicaraguan? His disproportionate, almost pathetic love for French symbolists and Parnassians, his vital cosmopolitanism, the touching devotion with which he read and admired the literary fashions of the time and insisted on adapting them to his own poetry, did not make his work simply derivative, an "underdeveloped and dependent poetry." Quite the contrary. With self-assured liberty, using everything within the cultural arsenal of his time that seduced his imagination, emotions, and instinct, melding the Spain of the Golden Century with his own Latin American experience, combining with remarkable irreverence the Greek philosophers and tragedians with licentious eighteenth-

century France courtesans, Rubén Darío led the
most profound revolution of Spanish-language poetry since the times of Góngora and Quevedo, rescu-
ing it from the traditional academicism where it had
languished and placing it once again, like the Spanish
poets of the sixteenth and seventeenth centuries, at
the vanguard of modernity.

Darío's case is like that of almost all great artists
and writers—Machado de Assis in Brazil, who never
would have written his lovely *comédie humaine* had
he not read Balzac's; Vallejo in Peru, whose poetry
made use of all the literary trends shaking up the literary life of Latin America and Europe between the
two world wars; in recent times, Octavio Paz in Mexico and Borges in Argentina. Borges' stories, essays,
and poems have surely had more influence on writers in other languages than any other contemporary
body of work in Spanish. More than anyone else, he
has contributed to making our literature respected
as creations of original ideas and forms. So, then,
would Borges' work have been possible without foreign "dependency"? Does the study of his influences
not take us through a variegated, fantastic cultural
geography, through far-flung continents, languages,
and historical ages? Borges is a transparent example
of how being a citizen of the world is the best way
to write an original work, to enrich the culture of

the nation in which one was born and the language in which one writes.

A country strengthens and develops its culture by opening its doors and windows wide to all intellectual, scientific, and artistic currents, encouraging the free flow of ideas, regardless of their origin, so that the native tradition and experiences are constantly tested and corrected, completed and enriched by those who, in other lands, with other languages and under different circumstances, share with us the miseries and grandeurs of the human adventure. Subjecting ourselves to that continual challenge and encouragement is the only way that our culture will become authentic, contemporary, and creative—and the best tool for our economic and social progress.

Condemning cultural nationalism for atrophying the spiritual life of a country does not in any way mean scorning national or regional traditions and modes of behavior, or denying that these serve, even in a primordial way, the country's thinkers, artists, technicians, and researchers in their work. It simply means demanding, in the realm of culture, the same liberty and pluralism that should be found in the politics and economics of a democratic society. The more diverse cultural life is, the richer it is and the freer and more intense the exchange and rivalry of ideas at its center.

Peruvians are in a privileged position to know

this, since our country is a cultural mosaic in which "all bloods" as Arguedas wrote, coexist or mix: the pre-Hispanic and Spanish cultures as well as all of the West that came to us with the Spanish language and history; the African presence, so alive in our music; the Asian migrations; and that collection of Amazon communities with their languages, legends, and traditions. These multiple voices speak equally for Peru, a pluralistic country, and none has more claim than any other to represent a "national essence."

We Peruvians see a similar abundance in our literature. Martín Adán, whose poetry does not seem to have any foundation or ambition other than language itself, is no more or less Peruvian than José María Eguren, who believed in fairies and revived characters of Nordic mythology in his small house in Barranco. José María Arguedas, who transfigured the Andean world in his novels, has no greater right to be considered a Peruvian author than César Moro, who wrote his most beautiful poems in French. Sometimes foreign influenced and sometimes folkloric, traditional at times and avant-garde at other times, from the coast, the highlands, or the jungle, realist or fantastic, with Spanish, French, Peruvian Indian, or North American influences, our literature expresses, in its contradictory personality, the complex and multiple truths of who we are.

Our literature became so expressive because it had the good fortune to develop with a freedom that flesh and blood Peruvians have not always enjoyed. In real life, our dictators were once so uncultured that they deprived men and women of their liberty but rarely of their books. But that was in the past. Today's dictatorships are ideological and seek to dominate not just our person but our spirit and ideas. That imperative explains why they claim that national culture must be protected against foreign infiltration. Using the excuse that they are defending the culture against the danger of "de-nationalization," they establish systems to control thoughts and words, when in truth they have no objective other than to squash criticism. With the argument of preserving the purity or ideological health of a native culture, the government assumes the role of director and warden of a country's intellectual and artistic production. When this occurs, cultural life becomes trapped in the straitjacket of bureaucracy.

This is unacceptable. To guarantee cultural liberty and pluralism, government's only legitimate role is to create optimal conditions for cultural life and to meddle as little as possible in that life as it takes shape. The government should guarantee freedom of expression and the free flow of ideas, foster research and the arts, and guarantee universal access to education and information. It should not impose or favor doctrines, theories, or ideologies but permit them to flourish and compete freely. I know it is difficult and almost utopian to expect such neutrality on the part of the modern state—an elephant so big and so clumsy that it causes damage by simply moving. But if we do not manage to control its movements and reduce them to the bare minimum, the state will end up trampling us.

Let us not repeat, today, the error of the Araucanian Indians—fighting alleged foreign enemies without realizing that the main obstacles we have to overcome are within ourselves. The cultural challenges we in Latin America face are too real and important for us to invent imaginary difficulties such as foreign powers bent on attacking and defiling our culture. We must not succumb to such persecution mania or to the demagogy of second-rate politicians who are convinced that anything goes in their struggle for power. For if they achieve this power, they will not hesitate to censor our creativity and suffocate it with dogmas designed to eliminate contradictions and opponents, as in Albert Camus' *Caligula*. In a vertiginous semantic shift, those who support such ideas call themselves progressives. But in reality they are reactionaries and contemporary obscurantists, perpetrators of that dark dynasty of jailers of the spirit, as Nietzsche called them, whose origins are lost in the night of human intolerance.

## Bibliography

Anderson, Benedict. *Imagined Communities: Reflections on the Origin and Spread of Nationalism*, rev. ed. London: Verso, 1983.

Berlin, Isaiah. *Vico and Herder: Two Studies in the History of Ideas.* London: Hogarth Press, 1976.

Espada, Arcadi. *Contra Catalunya: Una Crónica.* Barcelona: Flor del Viento Ediciones, 1997.

Gellner, Ernest. *Nations and Nationalism.* Oxford: Blackwell Publishers, 1983.

Hayek, Friedrich. *The Road to Serfdom.* 50th anniversary edition with a new introduction by Milton Friedman. Chicago: University of Chicago Press, 1994.

Juaristi, Jon. *El Bucle Melancólico: Historias de Nacionalistas Vascos.* Madrid: Editorial Espasa Calpe, 1997.

Kedouri, Elie. *Nationalism.* 4th ed. Oxford: Blackwell Publishers, 1981.

Popper, K. R. *The Open Society and Its Enemies,* vols. 1, 2. London: Routledge & Kegan Paul, 1986.

Savater, Fernando. "¿Tambores de paz?" *El País,* September 20, 1998.

Trías, Eugenio. "Aforismos para después de una tregua," *El Mundo,* October 3, 1998.

Vidal-Quadras, Aleix. *Amarás a Tu Tribu.* Barcelona: Editorial Planeta, 1998.

——— "El conjuro del exorcista," *El País,* February 16, 1998.

# 5

## FICTION AND REALITY
## IN LATIN AMERICA

The historian who mastered the subject of the discovery and conquest of Peru by the Spaniards better than anyone else had a tragic story: he died without having written the book for which he had prepared himself all his life and whose theme he knew so well that he almost gave the impression of being omniscient.

His name was Raúl Porras Barrenechea. He was a small, pot-bellied man, with a large forehead and a pair of blue eyes that became impregnated with malice every time he mocked someone. He was the most brilliant teacher I have ever had. Only Marcel Bataillon, another historian whom I had the chance to hear at the Collège de France (in a course of lectures he gave on a Peruvian chronicler, by the way), seemed to be able to match Porras Barrenechea's eloquence and evocative power as well as his academic integrity. But not even the learned and elegant Bataillon could captivate an audience with the enchantment of Porras Barrenechea. In the big old house of San Marcos, the first university founded by the Spaniards in the New World, a place that had already begun to fall into irreparable decay when I passed through it in the 1950s, the lectures on historical sources attracted such a vast number of listeners that it was necessary to arrive well in advance so as not to be left outside the classroom, listening together with dozens of students who were literally hanging from the doors and windows.

Whenever Porras Barrenechea spoke, history became anecdote, gesture, adventure, color, psychology. His depiction of history as a series of murals had the magnificence of a Renaissance painting. The determining factor of events was never impersonal forces—geographical imperative, economic relationships, divine providence—but a cast of certain outstanding individuals whose audacity, genius, charisma, or contagious insanity had imposed on each era and society a certain orientation and shape.

But along with this narrative concept of history, which the so-called scientific historians had already named as romantic in an effort to discredit it, Porras Barrenechea demanded knowledge and documentary precision, which none of his colleagues and critics at San Marcos has so far been able to equal. Those historians who dismissed Porras Barrenechea because he was interested in simple narrated history instead of a social or economic interpretation have been less effective than he was in explaining to us that crucial event in the destiny of Europe and America: the destruction of the Inca empire and the linking of its vast territories and peoples to the Western world. This was because for Porras Barrenechea, although history had to have a dramatic quality, architectonic beauty, suspense, richness, a wide range of human types, and the excellence in style of great fiction, everything in it also had to be scrupulously true, proven time after time.

In order to be able to narrate the discovery and conquest of Peru in this way, Porras Barrenechea, before anything else, had to evaluate very carefully all the witnesses and documents so as to establish the degree of credibility of each one of them. And in the numerous cases of deceitful testimonies, Porras Barrenechea had to find out the reasons that led the authors to conceal, misrepresent, or overpaint the facts so that, knowing their peculiar limitations, those sources had a double meaning: what they revealed and what they distorted. For forty years Porras Barrenechea dedicated all his powerful intellectual energy to this heroic hermeneutic. All the works he published while he was alive constituted the preliminary work for what should have been his *magnum opus*. Once he was perfectly equipped to embark upon it, pressing on with assurance through the labyrinthine jungle of chronicles, letters, testaments, rhymes, and ballads of discovery and conquest which he had read, cleansed, confronted, and almost memorized, sudden death put an end to his encyclopedic knowledge. As a result, all those interested in that era and in the people who lived in it have had to keep on reading the old but so far unsurpassed *History of the Conquest* written by an American, William Prescott, who never set foot in the country but who sketched it with extraordinary skill.

Dazzled by Porras Barrenechea's lectures, at one time I seriously considered the possibility of leaving aside literature so as to dedicate myself to history. Porras Barrenechea had asked me to work with him as an assistant in an ambitious project on the general history of Peru, under the auspices of the bookseller and publisher Juan Mejía Baca. It was Porras Barrenechea's task to write the volumes devoted to conquest and emancipation. For four years, I spent three hours a day, five days a week, in that dusty house on Colina Street, where the books, the card indexes, and the notebooks had slowly invaded and devoured everything, except Porras Barrenechea's bed and the dining table. My job was to read and take notes on the chroniclers' various themes, but principally on the myths and legends that preceded and followed the discovery and conquest of Peru. That experience has become an unforgettable memory for me. Anyone familiar with the chronicles of the conquest and discovery of America will understand why. They represent for us Latin Americans what the novels of chivalry represent for Europe: the beginning of literary fiction as we understand it today.

The novel was forbidden in the Spanish colonies by the inquisitors, who considered this literary genre to be as dangerous for the spiritual fate of the Indians as for the moral and political behavior of society. And in that opinion they were absolutely right. We novelists must be grateful to the Spanish Inquisition for having discovered, before any critic did, the inevitably subversive nature of fiction. The prohibition included reading and publishing novels in the colonies. There was no way, naturally, to avoid a great number of novels being smuggled into our countries, and we know, for example, that the first copies of *Don Quixote* entered America hidden in barrels of wine. We can only dream with envy about what kind of experience it was, in those times, in Spanish America, to read a novel: a sinful adventure in which, in order to abandon yourself to an imaginary world, you had to be prepared to face prison and humiliation.

Novels were not published in Spanish America until after the wars of independence. The first, *El Periquillo Sarniento (The Itching Parrot)*, appeared in Mexico only in 1816. Although novels were abolished for three centuries, the goal of the inquisitors—which was a society exonerated from the disease of fiction—was not achieved. They did not realize that the realm of fiction was larger and deeper than that of the novel. Nor could they imagine that the appetite for lies—that is, for escaping objective reality through illusions—was so powerful and rooted in the human spirit that, once the vehicle of the novel was not available to satisfy it, the thirst for fiction would infect, like a plague, all the other disciplines and genres in which the written word could freely flow. Repressing and censoring a literary genre that was specifically invented to give "the necessity of lying" a place in the culture, the inquisitors achieved the exact opposite of their intention: a world without novels, yes, but a world into which fiction spread and contaminated practically everything: history, religion, poetry, science, art, speeches, journalism, and daily habits.

We are still victims in Latin America of what we could call the revenge of the novel. We still have great difficulty in differentiating between fiction and reality. We are traditionally so accustomed to mixing them that this is probably one of the reasons why we are so impractical and inept in political matters. But some good also came from the novelization of our whole life. Books like *One Hundred Years of Solitude,* Cortázar's short stories, and Roa Bastos' novels would not have been possible otherwise.

The tradition from which this kind of literature sprang—in which we are exposed to a world totally reconstructed and subverted by fantasy—started, without doubt, in those chronicles of conquest and discovery that I read and noted under the guidance of Porras Barrenechea. History and literature—truth and falsehood, reality and fiction—mingle in these texts in a way that is often inextricable. The thin demarcation line that separates one from the other frequently fades away, so that both worlds can entwine in a completeness which, the more ambiguous it is, the more seductive it becomes, because the likely and unlikely in it seem to be part of the same substance.

Right in the middle of the most cruel battle, the Virgin appears, who, taking the believers' side, charges against the unlucky pagans. The shipwrecked conquistador Pedro Serrano actually lives out, on a tiny island in the Caribbean, the story of Robinson Crusoe, which a novelist only invented centuries later. The Amazons of Greek mythology materialize by the banks of the river baptized with their name, to wound Pedro de Orellana's followers with their arrows, one arrow landing in Fray Gaspar de Carvajal's buttocks, the man who meticulously narrated this event. Is that episode more fabulous than another, probably historically correct, one in which the poor soldier Manso de Leguisamo loses in one night of dice-playing the solid gold of the wall of the Temple of the Sun in Cuzco that was given to him in the spoils of war? Or more fabulous perhaps than the unutterable outrages committed—always with a smile on his face— by the rebel Francisco de Carvajal, that octogenarian Devil of the Andes who merrily began to sing: "Oh mother, my poor little curly hairs, the wind is taking them away one by one, one by one," as he was being taken to the gallows where he was to be hanged, quartered, beheaded, and burnt?

The chronicle distills fiction in life all the time, as in Borges' tale "Tlön, Uqbar, Orbis Teritus." Does this mean that its testimony must be challenged from a historical point of view and accepted only as literature? Not at all. Its exaggerations and fantasies often reveal more about the reality of the era than its truths. Astonishing miracles from time to time enliven the tedious pages of the *Crónica Moralizada (The Exemplary Chronicle)* of Padre Calancha, and sulfurous outrages come from the male and female demons fastidiously catechized in the Indian villages by the extirpators of idolatries, like Padre Arriaga, to justify their devastation of idols, amulets, ornaments, handicrafts, and tombs. These teach us more about the innocence, fanaticism, and stupidity of the time than the wisest of treaties. As long as one knows how to read them, everything is contained in these pages, written sometimes by men who hardly knew how to write but who were impelled by the unusual nature of contemporary events to try to record them for posterity, thanks to an intuition about the privilege they enjoyed: of being witness to and actors in events that were changing the history of the world. Because they narrate these events under the passion of recently lived experience, they often relate things that to us seem like naive or cynical fantasies. For the people of the time, they were not so, but phantoms that credulity, surprise, fear, and hatred had endowed with a solidity and vitality often more powerful than beings made of flesh and blood.

The conquest of Tahuantinsuyu—the empire of the Incas—by a handful of Spaniards is a fact of history that even now, after having digested and ruminated over all the explanations, we find hard to unravel. The first wave of conquistadors, Pizarro and his companions, were fewer than two hundred (not counting the black slaves and the collaborating Indians). When the reinforcements started to arrive, this first wave had already dealt a mortal blow to an empire that had ruled over at least twenty million people. This was not a primitive society, made up of barbaric tribes, like the ones the Spaniards had found in the Caribbean or in Darien, but a civilization that had reached a high level of social, military, agricultural, and handicraft development which, in many senses, Spain itself had not reached.

The most remarkable aspects of this civilization, however, were not the paths that crossed the four *suyos* or regions of its vast territory, the temples and fortresses, the irrigation systems or the complex administrative organization, but something in which all the testimonies of these chronicles coincide: this civilization managed to eradicate hunger in that immense region. It was able to produce—and distribute all that which was produced—in such a way that all its subjects had enough to eat. Only a very small number of empires throughout the history of the world have succeeded in achieving this.

Are the conquistadors' firearms, horses, and armor enough to explain the immediate collapse of this Inca civilization at the first clash with the Spaniards? It is true that gunpowder, bullets, and charging beasts were unknown to them, and the experience paralyzed the Indians with a religious terror and inspired in them the sensation that they were fighting not against men but against gods who were invulnerable to the arrows and slings with which they fought. Even so, the numerical difference was such that the Quechua Ocean would have had to shake in order to drown the invader. What prevented this from happening? What is the profound explanation for that defeat from which the Inca population never recovered?

The answer perhaps may lie hidden in the moving account of what happened in Cajamarca Square the day Pizarro captured the Inca Atahualpa. We must, above all, read the chronicles of those who were there, those who lived through the event or had direct testimony of it, like Pedro Pizarro. At the precise moment the emperor is captured, before the battle begins, his armies give up the fight as if manacled by a magic force. The slaughter is indescribable, but it comes from only one side: the Spaniards discharge their harquebuses, thrust their pikes and swords, and charge their horses against a bewildered mass, who, having witnessed the capture of their god and master, seem unable to defend themselves or even to run away. In the space of a few minutes, the army that had defeated Huáscar and had dominated all the northern provinces of the empire disintegrated like ice in warm water.

The vertical and totalitarian structure of the Tahuantinsuyu was, without doubt, more of a threat to its survival than all the conquistadors' firearms and iron weapons. As soon as the Inca, the figure who was the vortex toward which all wills converged, the axis around whom the entire society was organized and upon whom depended the inspiration and vitality, life and death, of every person, from the richest to the poorest, was captured, no one knew how to act. So—with heroism, we must admit—they did the only thing they could do without breaking the thousand and one taboos and precepts that regulated their existence: they let themselves get killed. And that was the fate of dozens and perhaps hundreds of Indians stultified by the confusion and loss of leadership they suffered when the Inca emperor, the life force of their universe, was captured right before their eyes.

Those Indians who let themselves be knifed or blown to pieces that somber afternoon in Cajamarca Square lacked the ability to make their own decisions, either with the sanction of the authority or indeed against it, and were incapable of taking individual initiative, of acting with a degree of independence according to changing circumstances. Those one hundred and eighty Spaniards who had placed the Indians in ambush and were now slaughtering them possessed this ability.

It was this difference, more than the numerical one or the weapons, that created an immense inequality between these two civilizations. The individual had no importance and virtually no existence in the Incas' pyramidal and theocratic society, the achievement of which had always been collective and anonymous: by carrying the gigantic stones of Machu Picchu citadel or of Ollantaytambo fortress up the steepest of peaks, directing water to all the slopes of the Cordillera hills by building terraces that even today enable irrigation to take place in the most desolate places, and making paths to unite regions separated by infernal geographies. A state religion that took away the individual's free will and crowned the authority's decision with the aura of a divine mandate turned the Tahuantinsuyu into a beehive: laborious, efficient, stoic. But its immense power was in fact very fragile; it rested completely on the sovereign-god's shoulders, the man whom the Indians had to serve and to whom they owed total and selfless obedience.

It was religion, rather than force, that preserved the people's metaphysical docility toward the Inca.

The creed and the rite, as well as the prohibitions and the feasts, the values and the vices, all served to strengthen the emperor's absolute power and to propitiate the expansionist and colonizing design of the Cuzco sovereigns. It was an essentially political religion, which on the one hand turned the Indians into diligent servants, and on the other was capable of receiving into its bosom, as minor gods, all the deities of the peoples that had been conquered—the idols of which were moved to Cuzco and enthroned by the Inca himself. The Inca religion was less cruel than the Aztec one, for it performed human sacrifices with a certain degree of moderation (if I can say this), making use of only the necessary cruelty to ensure the hypnosis and fear of the subjects toward the divine power incarnated in the temporary power of the Inca.

We cannot question the organizing genius of the Inca. The speed with which the empire, in the short period of a century, grew from its nucleus in Cuzco to become a civilization embracing three quarters of South America is incredible. And this was the result not only of the Quechuas' military efficiency but also of the Inca's ability to persuade the neighboring peoples and cultures to join the Tahuantinsuyu. Once they became part of the empire, the bureaucratic mechanism was immediately set in motion, enrolling the new servants in a system that dissolved individual life into a series of tasks and gregarian duties carefully programmed and supervised by the gigantic network of administrators whom the Inca sent to the farthest borders. Either to prevent or to extinguish rebelliousness, there was a system called *mitimaes,* whereby villages and people were removed *en masse* to faraway places where, feeling misplaced and lost, these exiles naturally assumed an attitude of passivity and absolute respect, which, of course, represented the Inca system's ideal citizen.

Such a civilization was capable of fighting against the natural elements and defeating them; it was capable of consuming rationally what it produced, heaping together reserves for future times of poverty or disaster; and it was also able to evolve slowly and with care in the field of knowledge, inventing only that which could support it and hindering all that which in some way or another could undermine its foundations (for example, writing or any other form of expression liable to encourage individual pride or a rebellious imagination). It was not capable, however, of facing the unexpected, that absolute novelty represented by a phalanx of armored men on horseback who assaulted the Incas with weapons, transgressing all the war and peace patterns known to them.

When, after the initial confusion, resistance started breaking out here and there, it was too late. The complicated machinery regulating the empire had entered a process of decomposition. Leaderless with the murder of Huayna Cápac's two sons—Huáscar, whose killing was ordered by his brother Atahualpa, who was in turn executed by Pizarro—the Inca system fell into a monumental state of confusion and cosmic deviation, similar to the chaos which, according to the Cuzquean sages, the Amautas, had prevailed in the world before the Tahuantinsuyu was founded by Manco Cápac and Mama Ocllo. While caravans of Indians loaded with gold and silver continued taking to the conquistadors the treasures the Inca had ordered to be brought to pay for his rescue, a group of Quechua generals, attempting to organize resistance, fired at the wrong target: because of their grudge against their ancient Indian masters they vented their fury on the groups that had begun to collaborate with the Spaniards.

Spain had already won the game, although the rebellious outbreaks (which were always localized and counterchecked by the servile obedience that great sectors of the Inca system transferred automatically to their new masters) had multiplied in the following years, up to Manco Inca's insurrection. But not even these, however important, represented a real danger to Spanish rule.

Those who destroyed the Inca empire and created a country they called Peru—a country which four and a half centuries later has not yet managed to heal the bleeding wounds of its birth—were men whom we can hardly admire. They were, it is true, uncommonly courageous, but, in opposition to what the edifying stories teach us, most of them lacked any idealism or higher purpose. They possessed only greed, hunger, and, in the best of cases, a certain penchant for adventure. The cruelty in which the Spaniard took pride—and which the chronicles depict to the point of making us shiver—was inscribed in the ferocious customs of the times and was, without doubt, equivalent to that of the people they subdued and almost extinguished (three centuries later the Inca population had been reduced from twenty million to only six million).

But these semi-literate, implacable, and greedy swordsmen who, even before having completely conquered the Inca empire, were already savagely fighting among themselves, or fighting the "pacifiers" sent against them by the faraway monarch to whom they had given a continent, represented a culture in which (we will never know if for the benefit or disgrace of mankind) something new, exotic, had germinated in the history of man. In this culture, although injustice and abuses proliferated, often favored by religion, little by little, in an unforeseen way, by the alliance of multiple factors—not least among them chance—a social space of human activities had opened up that was neither legislated nor controlled by the powers. This would produce the most extraordinary economic, scientific, and technical developments human civilization has ever known, since the times of cavemen with their clubs; and it would also give way to the creation of the individual as the sovereign source of values that society had to respect.

These who, rightly so, are shocked by the abuses and crimes of the Spanish conquest must bear in mind that the first men to condemn them and ask that they be brought to an end were men like Padre Las Casas, who came to America with the conquistadors and abandoned their ranks in order to collaborate with the defeated ones, whose sufferance of their oppressors they denounced with an indignation and virulence that still moves us today. Padre Las Casas was the most active, although not the only one, of those nonconformists who rebelled against the abuses inflicted upon the Indians. They fought against their fellow men and against the policies of

their own country in the name of a moral principle which to them was a higher authority than any
nation or state. This could not have been possible
among the Inca or any of the other pre-Hispanic cultures. In these cultures, as in the other great historical civilizations foreign to the West, the individual
could not morally question the social organism of
which he was part, because he existed only as an integral atom of that organism, and because for him
the reasoning of the state could not be separated
from morality.

The first culture to interrogate and question itself,
the first to break up the masses into individual beings
who, with time, gradually gained the right to think
and act for themselves, was to become—thanks to
that unknown exercise, freedom—the most powerful
civilization in the world. It is useless to ask oneself
whether it was good that it happened in this manner
or whether it would have been better for humanity if
the individual had never been born and the tradition
of the antlike societies had continued for ever.

The pages of the chronicles of conquest and discovery in Latin America depict that crucial, bloody
moment full of phantasmagoria in which—disguised
as a handful of invading treasure-hunters, killing and
destroying—the Judeo-Christian tradition, the Spanish language, Greece, Rome, and the Renaissance,

the notion of individual sovereignty, and the chance of living sometime in freedom reached the shores of the Empire of the Sun.

So it was that we Peruvians were born. And, also, of course, the Bolivians, Chileans, Ecuadorians, Colombians, and so on. Almost five centuries later this is still an unfinished business. We have not yet, properly speaking, seen the light. We do not yet constitute real nations. Our contemporary reality is still impregnated with the violence and marvels that those first texts of our literature—those novels disguised as history and historical books corrupted by fiction—told us about. At least one basic problem is the same. Two cultures, one Western and modern, the other aboriginal and archaic, hardly coexist, separated one from the other because of the exploitation and discrimination of the former toward the latter. Our country—our countries—are in a deep sense more a fiction than a reality.

In the eighteenth century, in France, the name of Peru rang with a golden echo, and an expression was then born—*ce n'est pas le Pérou* [It is not Peru]—which is used when something is not as rich and extraordinary as its legendary name suggests. Well, *Le Pérou, ce n'est pas le Pérou!* It never was, at least for the great part of its inhabitants, that fabulous country of legends and fictions, but rather an artificial gathering of men with different languages, customs, and traditions whose only common denominator was having been condemned by history to live together without knowing or loving one another.

The immense opportunities brought by the civilization that discovered and conquered America have been beneficial only to a minority—sometimes a very small one—whereas the great majority manage to receive only the negative share of the conquest— that is, contributing through their serfdom and sacrifice, misery and neglect, to the prosperity and refinement of the Westernized elites.

One of our worst defects—and one of our best fictions—is to believe that our miseries have been imposed on us from abroad, that others have always had the responsibility for our problems; for instance, the conquistadors. There are countries in Latin America—Mexico is the best example—in which the "Spaniards" are even more severely indicted for what "they" did to the Indians. Did "they" really do it? We did it. We are the conquistadors. "They" were our own parents and grandparents who came to these shores and gave us the habit of passing to the devil the responsibility for any evil we do in the world. Instead of making amends for what they did, by improving and correcting our relationship with our indigenous compatriots, mixing with them and amalgamating ourselves to form a new culture that would have been a kind of synthesis of the best of both, we—the Westernized Latin Americans—have persevered in the worst habits of our forebears, behaving toward the Indians during the nineteenth and twentieth centuries as the Spaniards behaved toward the Aztecs and Incas. And sometimes even worse. We must remember that in countries like Chile and Argentina it was during the republican period, not the colonial, that the native cultures were systematically exterminated. It is a fact that in many of our countries, as in Peru, we share, in spite of the pious and hypocritical "indigenist" rhetoric of our men of letters and politicians, the mentality of the conquistadors.

Only in countries where the native population was small or nonexistent, or where the aboriginals were practically liquidated, can we talk of integrated societies. In the others, a discreet, sometimes unconscious but very effective apartheid prevails. There, integration is extremely slow and the price the indigenous peoples have to pay for it is high: renunciation of their culture—their language, beliefs, traditions, and customs—and adoption of the culture of their ancient masters.

Maybe there is no realistic way to integrate our societies other than by asking the Indians to pay that price. Maybe the ideal—that is, the preservation of the primitive cultures of America—is a utopia incompatible with this other and more urgent goal: the establishment of societies in which social and economic inequalities among citizens are reduced to human, reasonable limits and where everybody can enjoy a decent and free life. In any case, we have been unable to reach any of those ideals and are still, as when we had just entered Western history, trying to find what we are and what our future will be.

That is why it is very useful for Latin Americans to review the literature that gives testimony to discovery and conquest. In these chronicles we not only dream about the time in which our fantasy and our realities seemed to be incestuously confused; in them we also learn about the roots of our problems and challenges that are still there, unanswered. And in these half-literary, half-historical pages we also perceive, formless, mysterious, fascinating, the promise of something new and formidable, something that, if it ever would turn into reality, would enrich the world and improve civilization.

Of this promise we have had, until now, only sporadic manifestations—in our literature and in our art, for example. But it is not only in our fictions that we must strive to achieve; we must not stop until our promise passes from our dreams and words into our daily lives and becomes objective reality. We must not permit our countries to disappear, as did my dear teacher, the historian Porras Barrenechea, without writing in real life the definitive masterwork we have been preparing ourselves to accomplish since the three caravels stumbled onto our coasts.

# 6

## ISAIAH BERLIN,
## A HERO OF OUR TIME

Many years ago, I read in Spanish translation a book on Karl Marx which was so clear, suggestive, and unprejudiced that I spent a long time looking for other books by its author, Isaiah Berlin. I later discovered that until recently his work had been difficult to find since it was scattered, if not buried, in academic publications. With the exception of his books on Vico and Herder, and the four essays on freedom, which were available in the English-language world, most of his work had led the quiet life of the library and the specialist journal. But that was before a former student of his, Henry Hardy, collected his essays together in four volumes: *Russian Thinkers, Against the Current, Concepts and Categories,* and *Personal Impressions.*

This was an important event, because Isaiah

Berlin—a Latvian brought up and educated in England, where he was a professor of social and political theory at Oxford and president of the Royal Academy—was one of the most exceptional minds of our time. He was a political thinker and essayist of extraordinary breadth whose work provides a rare pleasure in its skill and brilliance as well as offering an invaluable guide for understanding, in all their complexity, the moral and historical problems faced by human societies.

Berlin believed passionately in ideas, and in the influence that ideas have on the behavior of individuals and groups. Yet, at the same time, as a good pragmatist, he was aware of the space that usually opens up between ideas and the words that seek to express them, and between the words and the deeds that purport to put them into practice. Despite their intellectual density, his essays never seem abstract to us—unlike, for example, the works of Michel Foucault and the later works of Roland Barthes—or the result of a speculative and rhetorical virtuosity that has, at some moment, cut its moorings with reality. Instead, Berlin's essays are deeply rooted in common experience. The collection entitled *Russian Thinkers* is an epic fresco of intellectual and political thought in nineteenth-century Russia; yet the most outstanding characters are not people but ideas. These shine, move around, challenge one another, and change with the vigor of heroes in an adventure novel. In that other beautiful book on a similar theme—*To the Finland Station* by Edmund Wilson—the thoughts of the protagonists seem to transpire from the persuasive and varied portraits that the author draws of his characters. Here, by contrast, it is the concepts that they formulated, the ideals and arguments with which they confronted one another, their intuitions and knowledge, which define the figures of Tolstoy, Herzen, Belinski, Bakunin, and Turgenev and make them plausible or reprehensible.

But even more than *Russian Thinkers,* the collection *Against the Current* will doubtless remain Isaiah Berlin's major contribution to the culture of our time. Each essay in this magisterial work reads like a chapter of a novel whose action takes place in the world of thought and in which the heroes and the villains are ideas. Thanks to this scholar who never loses a sense of balance and who can clearly see the wood for the trees, Machiavelli, Vico, Montesquieu, Hume, Sorel, Marx, Disraeli, and even Verdi are seen to have a great contemporary significance, and the things they believed, put forward, or criticized illuminate in a powerful way the political and social conflicts that we wrongly considered to be specific to our age.

The most surprising thing about this thinker is

that he appears, at first sight, not to offer ideas of his own. It might seem nonsense to say this, but it is not nonsense because when one reads him, one has the impression that in these essays Berlin achieves what, after Flaubert (and because of him), most modern novelists have tried to achieve in their novels: to erase themselves, to make themselves invisible, to offer the illusion that their stories are self-generated. There are many techniques for making the narrator disappear in a novel. The technique that Berlin uses to make us feel that he is not behind his texts is "fair play." This is the scrupulous attention with which he analyses, exhibits, summarizes, and quotes the thoughts of his subjects, considering all their arguments, weighing the extenuating circumstances they faced, the constraints of the age, never pushing the words or ideas of others in one direction or another to make them appear similar to his own. This objectivity in the transmission of the invention of others gives rise to the fantastic impression that, in these books which say so many things, Isaiah Berlin himself has nothing of his own to say.

This is, of course, a rigorously false impression. "Fair play" is only a technique which, like all narrative techniques, has just one function: to make the content more persuasive. A story that seems not to be told by anyone in particular, which pretends to be creating itself, by itself, at the moment of reading, can often be more plausible and engrossing for the reader. A thought that seems not to exist by itself, that reaches us indirectly, through what certain eminent men from different epochs and cultures thought at specific moments in their life, or one that professes to be born not out of the creative effort of an individual mind but rather out of the contrast between the philosophical and political conceptions of others and the gaps and errors in these conceptions, can be more convincing than a thought that is presented, simply and arrogantly, as a single theory. The discretion and modesty of Isaiah Berlin are, in fact, a wily stratagem.

He was a "reformist" philosopher, a defender of individual sovereignty, convinced both of the need for change and social progress and of the inevitable concessions that the latter demands of the former. He was a believer in freedom as an alternative undertaking for individuals and nations, although he was aware of the obligations that economic, cultural, and political conditions bring to bear on this option. He was also a clear defender of pluralism, that is, of tolerance and the coexistence of different ideas and forms of life, and a resolute opponent of any form of despotism, be it intellectual or social. My description of him, with its generalizations and abstractions, obviously says something about the man, but it also, to some extent, deprives the reader of the pleasure of discovering these ideas through that lingering, subtle, and indirect method—a novelist's method—that Berlin uses to expound his convictions.

Some years back, I lost my taste for political utopias, those apocalypses that promise to bring heaven down to earth. I now know that they usually lead to injustices as serious as those they hope to put right. Since then, I have thought that common sense is the most valuable of political virtues. Reading Isaiah Berlin, I have come to see clearly something that I had intuited in a confused way: real progress, which has withered or overthrown barbarous practices and institutions that once were the source of infinite suffering for humankind and has established more civilized relations and styles of life, has always been achieved through a partial, heterodox, and deformed application of social theories. Social theories *in the plural,* which means that different, sometimes irreconcilable, ideologies have brought about identical or similar forms of progress. The prerequisite was always that these systems should be flexible and could be amended and reformed when they moved from the abstract to the concrete and came up against the daily experience of human beings. The filter at work which separates what is desirable from what is

not desirable in these systems is the criterion of practical reason. It is a paradox that someone like Isaiah
Berlin, who loved ideas so much and moved among
them with such ease, was always convinced that it is
ideas that must give way if they come into contradiction with human reality, since if the reverse occurs,
the streets are filled with guillotines and firing-squad
walls and the reign of the censors and the policemen
begins.

A constant in Western thought is the belief that
one true answer exists for every human problem, and
that once we find this answer, then all others must
be rejected as mistaken. A complementary idea, as
old as this one, is that the most noble and inspiring
ideas—justice, freedom, peace, pleasure, and so on—
are compatible with one another. For Isaiah Berlin,
these two beliefs are false, and many of the trage-
dies that have befallen humanity can be laid at their
doorstep. From this skeptical base, Berlin produced a
number of powerful and original arguments in favor
of freedom of choice and ideological pluralism.

Faithful to his indirect method, Isaiah Berlin sets
out his theory of contradictory truths, or of irreconcilable ends, by analyzing other thinkers who have
shown intimations of this thesis. Thus, for example,
in his essay on Machiavelli, he tells us that Machiavelli detected, in an involuntary, casual way, this "un-

comfortable truth" that not all values are necessarily compatible, that the idea of a single, definitive philosophy underpinning a perfect society is materially and conceptually impossible. Machiavelli reached this conclusion by studying the mechanisms of power in his own time, and discovering that they were at variance with the values of Christianity that, nominally, regulated communal life. To lead a "Christian life" and to apply rigorously the ethical norms laid down by that belief system meant condemning oneself to political impotence, at the mercy of unscrupulous and calculating people. If one wanted to be politically adept and construct a "glorious" community like Athens or Rome, then one had to replace Christian education with something more appropriate to that desired end. For Berlin, what was important was not so much that Machiavelli had pointed out this dilemma between a Christian life and a politically influential life; rather, it was his intuition that both aspects of the dilemma were equally persuasive and tempting from a moral and a social point of view. The author of *The Prince* saw that men and women could be torn between aspirations that were equally appealing and yet incompatible.

Every social utopia—from Plato to Marx—is founded on an act of faith: the belief that human ideals, the great aspirations of individuals and societies, can be harmonized, that achieving one or several of these goals does not preclude achieving others. Perhaps nothing expresses this optimism better than the rhythmic motto of the French Revolution: "Liberty, Equality, Fraternity." That well-intentioned movement, which sought to establish a government of reason on earth and put into practice these simple and unquestionable ideals, demonstrated to the world, through repeated slaughter and frustration, that social reality was more tumultuous and unpredictable than French philosophers had supposed when they prescribed this impeccably abstract recipe for human happiness. Instead of being mutually supportive, liberty, equality, and fraternity sabotaged one another at the very moment they moved from theory into practice.

The French revolutionaries discovered, to their surprise, that liberty was a generator of inequality—that a country whose citizens had complete or extensive freedom of initiative and control over their own actions and wealth would sooner or later develop material and spiritual imbalances. In order to maintain equality, there was no option but to sacrifice liberty and impose the coercion and surveillance of an all-powerful state whose policies would level out these social inequities. That social injustice was the price of liberty, that dictatorship was the price of equality, and that fraternity could be achieved only in a relative and transitory fashion, as when a war or some other catastrophe brought people together— these were the sad and difficult facts revealed by the French Revolution.

For Isaiah Berlin, what is worse than accepting the terrible dilemma of contradictory truths is refusing to accept it. For however tragic this reality might be, it allows us, in practical terms, to learn worthwhile lessons. The philosophers, historians, and political thinkers who have intuited this concept have been better able to understand the process of civilization. For example, Montesquieu, through a different route from that of Machiavelli, saw that the many different goals of men and women were often incompatible, and that these incompatibilities were the cause of conflicts between civilizations and disputes between different nations. They also led to rivalries between classes and groups within a single society, and even to crises and anguish within individuals themselves.

Like Montesquieu in the eighteenth century, the great Russian writer and nonconformist Alexander Herzen understood this dilemma in the nineteenth century, and this allowed him to analyze with greater lucidity than his contemporaries the failure of the European revolutions of 1848 and 1849. Herzen is one of Berlin's favored spokesmen. The affinities between the two thinkers are great, and Berlin has written one of his most brilliant essays on this philosopher. The skepticism they share has a curiously positive and stimulating effect: it becomes a call to action because it is both pragmatic and, at times, optimistic. Herzen was one of the first philosophers to reject the idea that humanity has a splendid future ahead and that current generations should be sacrificed to achieve it. Like Herzen, Berlin often reminds us that no justice has ever stemmed from political injustice and that liberty has never been born out of oppression. For that reason, both men believe that in social issues, small but effective achievements are always preferable to great, all-encompassing solutions, which they condemn as illusory.

The fact that there are contradictory truths, that human ideals can be in conflict, does not mean, according to Berlin, that we should despair and feel powerless. It means that we must be aware of the importance of freedom of choice. In the absence of one answer to our problems, we must be ever alert, testing the ideas, laws, and values that govern our world, comparing them and weighing the impact they have on our lives, choosing some and rejecting or modifying the rest. And while this is an argument in favor of responsibility and freedom of choice, Berlin also sees it as an irrefutable argument for tolerance and pluralism not just as moral imperatives but as practical requirements for the survival of humankind. If we accept that we ourselves must reject some truths and ends in order to pursue others— that our own internal values are, at times, in conflict—then this argues for tolerance when other people make choices different from our own. We must also admit that diversity—of ideas, actions, customs, morals, and cultures—is the only guarantee we have that if error becomes enshrined, the havoc it causes will be contained, because we have not one but many solutions to our problems, all of them precarious and provisional.

Liberty is a key concept in Isaiah Berlin's pursuit of tolerance and pluralism, and he contributed two concepts to help clarify this protean notion: negative liberty and positive liberty. Although the distinction is subtle and somewhat elusive when approached theoretically, the difference between these two forms of freedom becomes very clear when we assess concrete options, historical situations, and specific policies. And the difference also throws into relief problems that are often hidden by artificial divisions such as "formal" and "real" liberty—a distinction people usually make when they are looking to suppress "formal" liberty.

Liberty is closely linked to constraint. We are freer to the extent that we find less obstacles in the way of organizing our lives according to our own criteria. The less authority imposed on my actions—the more I can choose from among my own motivations (my needs, ambitions, and personal fantasies) without the interference of outside forces—the freer I am. This is the "negative" concept of liberty.

This concept focuses on the individual, and it is absolutely modern. It develops in societies that have achieved a high level of civilization and a certain degree of affluence. It is based on the supposition that the sovereignty of the individual must be respected because personal freedom is, in the final instance, the source of human creativity, intellectual and artistic development, and scientific progress. If the individual is suffocated, conditioned, and mechanized, then that wellspring of creativity is cut off, and the result is a gray and mediocre world, peopled by ants or robots. Those who embrace this idea of liberty believe that power and authority pose the greatest danger to society, but since authority and power are inevitable, they argue, their sphere of influence should be kept to a minimum—just what is necessary to avoid the break up of society—and that they should be scrupulously regulated and controlled.

Philosophers like John Stuart Mill and Benjamin

Constant formulated this concept of liberty with the greatest passion, and nineteenth-century liberalism was its most evident political expression. But it would be wrong to think that negative liberty ends there. In fact, it covers something much greater, more diverse, and more permanent; it is the underlying assumption of countless political programs, intellectual initiatives, and forms of behavior. This negative concept of liberty informs all democratic theories, in which the coexistence of different points of view or creeds is essential, along with respect for minority opinions. It also encourages the conviction that freedom of the press, religion, occupation, and movement—and, today, freedom of sexual behavior—must be safeguarded, for without these liberties life becomes impoverished and degraded.

Ideas as disparate as literary romanticism, monasticism, mysticism, anarchism, social democracy, the market economy, and liberal philosophy are connected, despite their obvious discrepancies, by the stake they all have in the concept of negative liberty. But in the political arena, it is not just democratic systems that bring about such freedom. Berlin shows that, however paradoxical it might seem, certain dictatorships that are repugnant to us can accommodate negative liberty and even put it into practice. We have witnessed this in Latin America, just as

Spaniards witnessed it during Franco's final years. Certain right-wing dictatorships that emphasize economic freedoms, despite the abuses and crimes they commit, often guarantee a wider margin of negative freedom to their citizens than do socialist or socialist-leaning democracies.

While negative liberty wants to limit authority, positive liberty looks to take control of, and exert, authority. The focus here is on the society rather than the individual, based on the (very fair) idea that each individual's possibility for realizing his or her own potential is largely determined by "social" causes beyond any one person's control. How can an illiterate person benefit from freedom of the press? What use is freedom of movement to someone living in dire poverty? Does freedom to work mean the same to the owner of a factory as to someone who is unemployed? While negative liberty mainly concentrates on the fact that individuals have different motivations and desires, positive liberty emphasizes their similarities and shared needs. The one argues that liberty is preserved by respecting variants and particular cases, the other that liberty is increased when there are fewer differences in society, when a community is more homogeneous.

Ideologies and beliefs that are all-embracing and are convinced that there is one ultimate, unique goal for a given community—a nation, a race, a class. or the whole of humanity—share this positive concept of liberty. It has brought mankind a great number of benefits, and thanks to it we have a social consciousness: an awareness that drastic economic, social, and cultural inequalities are an evil that can and must be corrected. Notions of human solidarity, social responsibility, and justice have been enriched and expanded thanks to the positive concept of freedom, which has also served to curb or abolish abuses ranging from slavery to racism and discrimination.

But this concept of liberty has also generated its own abuses. Just as General Pinochet and General Franco (in his "liberal" years) could speak, with some justification, of promoting negative liberty, so Hitler and Stalin could state, without too much exaggeration, that their respective regimes were establishing true (positive) freedom in their nations. All social utopias, left or right wing, religious or secular, are based on a positive notion of liberty. They are convinced that in every person there is, alongside a specific, distinct individual, something much more important: a social "I" who aspires to a collective ideal, and who is willing to sacrifice any impediment to that ideal's realization. In the name of this "positive" liberty—this future utopia, or the triumph of the chosen race, or a society without classes and states, or the city of the blessed—asphyxiating regimes have come to power, all forms of dissidence and criticism have been eliminated, concentration camps have been set up, millions of human beings have been exterminated, and the most cruel wars have been fought.

These two concepts of liberty are at odds with each other, they mutually reject each other, but there is no sense in trying to demonstrate that one is true and the other false. This is one of those cases of contradictory truths or incompatible goals that, according to Berlin, underlie our human condition. In theory, one can stack up an infinite number of arguments in favor of one or the other concept of liberty, all equally valid or questionable. But in practice—in social life, in history—the ideal is to try to achieve some kind of transaction between the two. The societies that have managed to achieve a compromise between these two forms of liberty have achieved a more decent and just (or less indecent and less unjust) standard of living. But this is a very difficult and precarious transaction because, as Isaiah Berlin points out, "negative" and "positive" liberty are not two interpretations of a concept, but something more: two profoundly divergent and irreconcilable attitudes toward human development.

Among the preserved fragments from the Greek poet Archilochus, there is one that says: "The fox knows many things, but the hedgehog knows one, big, thing." This formula, according to Isaiah Berlin, can serve to isolate two kinds of thinkers: artists and human beings in general. There are those who possess a central, systematized vision of life, an organizing principle that makes sense of, and assembles into a structure, historical events and everyday actions, the individual and society. There are others who have a dispersed and multiple view of reality and of men and women, which they do not form into a coherent explanation or order because they see the world as complex and diverse, where specific acts or events might have their own logic and coherence, but where the whole is tumultuous, contradictory, and ungraspable. The first of these is a "centripetal" view, the latter a "centrifugal" view. Dante, Plato, Hegel, Dostoyevsky, Nietzsche, and Proust are, according to Berlin, hedgehogs. The foxes are Shakespeare, Aristotle, Montaigne, Molière, Goethe, Balzac, and Joyce.

Berlin himself is, without doubt, one of the foxes. Not just for his open, pluralist vision of humanity but also because of the cunning with which he presents his formidable intuitions and intellectual discoveries: indirectly, as simple rhetorical figures slipped into lectures, or as mere working hypotheses. The metaphor of the hedgehog and the fox occurs at the beginning of one of his most compelling essays, on

Tolstoy's theory of history and its similarities with that of the conservative thinker Joseph de Maistre. As soon as Berlin formulates the metaphor, he is quick to warn us against the dangers of any classification of this sort. For these can indeed be artificial and even absurd.

But not in his case. Quite the reverse. Here, the metaphor is as illuminating a way of understanding two attitudes toward life that are present in all fields of culture—philosophy, literature, politics, and science—as his distinction between negative and positive liberty was in explaining the problem of freedom. A "centripetal" view explicitly or implicitly reduces everything that happens and everything that is to a well-wrought nucleus of ideas, through which the chaos of life becomes order and the opacity of things becomes transparent. This view has been based at times on faith, as in the case of Saint Augustine or Saint Thomas, and in other instances on reason, as in the work of Sade, Marx, or Freud. And despite the very great differences in form, content, and intention (and, of course, in talent) among these different writers, there is a kinship among them. This is their all-encompassing viewpoint which, they believe, allows them to identify and structure all experiences. This instrument, this key—grace, the unconscious, sin, the social relations of production, desire—offers the general structure that underpins life and also the framework within which men and women develop, suffer, or find pleasure, as well as offering an explanation of why and how they act in this way. From the hedgehog's point of view, chance, accident, and arbitrary events disappear from the world, or assume insignificance.

Unlike this world in which generalities are the norm, the fox is confined to the particular. For the fox, the "general" does not exist: there are only particular cases, so many and so diverse that bringing them together does not lead to any significant unity but rather to dizzying confusion, a magma of contradictions. The literary examples that Berlin provides, Shakespeare and Balzac, are typical. The work of both these writers offers an extraordinarily dynamic range of individuals who bear no resemblance to one another in terms of their private intentions or their public actions, a vast panoply of different behaviors and moral outlook. Critics that try to isolate "constants" in these worlds and offer a unifying vision of their characters and their lives leave us with the distinct impression that they are impoverishing or betraying the work of Shakespeare and Balzac. For these writers did not have one viewpoint; they had several, contradictory, viewpoints.

Whether it is disguised or explicit, in every hedgehog there is a fanatic, in every fox, a skeptic. Those who believe that they have found a final explanation for the world end up barricading themselves within this explanation and not wanting to learn of any others. Thanks to hedgehogs, extraordinary deeds have been undertaken—discoveries, conquests, revolutions—because for this type of glorious enterprise one inevitably needs the zeal and heroism that the centripetal viewpoint often inspires in its followers. Thanks to the foxes, our "quality" of life has improved, because people who are unwilling to accept that there is a single, unique explanation for life, and tacitly admit that there are different, dissimilar outlooks on life, find it much easier to countenance, and sometimes structure their lives around, ideas of tolerance, mutual respect, permissiveness, and freedom.

There are certain arenas in which hedgehogs have naturally predominated: in politics, for example, where all-embracing, clear, and coherent answers to problems are always more popular and—apparently, at least—more effective when it comes to governing a country. In the arts and literature, by contrast, the foxes are more numerous (but not so much in the sciences, where they remain a minority). Berlin shows that in the case of Tolstoy, a hedgehog and a fox can coexist in the same person. This remarkable novelist of the "particular," this prodigious observer of human diversity, who described all the different individual cases that comprise society, this fierce challenger of the abstractions offered by historians and philosophers who endeavored to explain human development in terms of a rational system—Tolstoy the fox—was hypnotically tempted by the ambition of achieving a unified, central view of life, and managed this, first with the historical determinism of *War and Peace,* and more notably in the prophetic religious phase of his final years.

I think that the case of Tolstoy is not unique—that all of us foxes always envy the hedgehogs. For hedgehogs, life is much more livable. Although the vicissitudes of life fall identically on both groups, for some mysterious reason suffering and dying are less difficult and intolerable—and sometimes easier—for those people who feel that they possess a central universal truth, a gleaming cog within the machine that we call life, a cog that knows its function within the whole. But the existence of foxes is also a constant challenge to hedgehogs, the siren song that confused Ulysses. Because although it is much easier to live in clarity and order, there is an irremediable human facet that looks to deny such simplicity and, quite often, seeks out the shadows and disorder.

What influence does the individual have in history? Are the great collective events, the development of humankind, the result of impersonal forces, of social mechanisms over which isolated people have little or no influence? Or (the opposite point of view) is everything that happens fundamentally the result of the vision, the genius, the fantasy, and the exploits of particular men and women? These are the questions that Isaiah Berlin addresses in the essays collected in the volume *Personal Impressions*.

The book contains fourteen texts, dating between 1948 and 1980, mainly in praise of politicians, academics, and writers, penned to be read at university ceremonies or published in journals. Despite their occasional nature, and the fact that some were written to fulfill an obligation, they are all very elegant and intelligent, displaying the vast erudition and the stimulating insights of his best essays. As a whole, they comprise a gallery of representative figures, which Berlin considers to be the most admirable and worthy of respect of his contemporaries, his personal anthology of heroes of our time. The most immediate impression the reader takes from this curious and sometimes unexpected fellowship—where celebrities like Churchill and Pasternak rub shoulders with unknown Oxford bibliophiles—is that, as Berlin says of one of his models (Einstein): if we are going to pay homage to certain individuals, it should be to those who have achieved something important in the field of knowledge and culture rather than in areas of conquest and power.

Between the individualist, romantic view of history and the collectivist, abstract view of the positivists and socialists, it is clear that Berlin is resolutely in favor of the former. But as always, his argument is nuanced, because, for him, any rigidly unilateral position is unthinkable. He does not deny that there are "objective forces" in social processes. But as his articles on Churchill, Roosevelt, and Chaim Weizmann argue explicitly, he has no doubt that the intervention of individuals—leaders, ideologues—in history is both fundamental and decisive. And that these individuals can push the "objective forces" into the background, often shaping the development of a people, modeling their behavior, and instilling in them the energy, determination, and spirit of sacrifice to defend certain causes and bring about specific policies. The formidable and, for a long period, the solitary resistance of the British against Nazism would not have been the same without Churchill. The United States' New Deal—that great social experiment in egalitarianism and democracy—would not have been what it was without Roosevelt. Modern Zionism and the creation of Israel would not have turned out the way it did without Chaim Weizmann.

Berlin is only too aware of the terrible distortions that the concept of the hero in history has suffered, the demagogy that surrounds it, from Carlyle's study to the hagiographies of absolute leaders who are seen to personify their people, like Hitler, Stalin, Franco, Mussolini, Mao, and so many other little demigods of our time. It is precisely his convinced anti-totalitarianism that leads him to emphasize that his three "heroes" are admirable for the most part because, although they were great men, with an extraordinary ability to influence their fellow citizens, they always worked within a democratic framework and the constraints of law, tolerant of criticism and obedient to the ballot box. It is this shared quality of leaders who are respectful of law and liberty that, for Berlin, unites the conservative Churchill, the democrat Roosevelt, and the liberal Weizmann over and above their doctrinal differences.

But history is not just made up of politicians and does not draw just on objective facts. In Berlin's civil pantheon, educators—all those who produce, criticize, or disseminate ideas—are given a privileged position. As in his other books, we see here clearly Berlin's conviction that these people are the motor force of life, the backdrop on which all social events are inscribed, and the key for understanding both outer reality and inner lives. That is why he expresses unreserved enthusiasm for Einstein, who radically transformed our understanding of the physical world, and Aldous Huxley, Maurice Bowra, and the poets Anna Akhmatova and Boris Pasternak, who spiritually enriched the time they lived in, questioning established intellectual values and exploring new critical issues, or creating works whose beauty and depth give both pleasure and understanding to us all.

Isaiah Berlin was a moralist as well as a convinced rationalist. Although he did not say this in so many words, it is clear from these glowing portraits that, for him, it is difficult, perhaps impossible, to disassociate the intellectual and artistic greatness of individuals from their ethical stance. All the individuals that populate these reverential pages are seen as positive both intellectually and morally—to such an extent that the two terms seem to be, for Berlin, synonymous. It is true that some of these exemplary figures, like the historian L. B. Namier, have psychological difficulties and appear at times insufferable, but all of them, deep down, display noble feelings and are generous, decent, and upright in their dealings. Isaiah Berlin is so persuasive that, when we read him, we are even inclined to believe that talent and virtue go together. But is this the case?

Of the authors that I have read in the recent past, Berlin is the one who has impressed me the most. His philosophical, historical, and political opinions seem to me illuminating and instructive. However, I feel that although perhaps few people in our time have seen in such a penetrating way what life is—the life of the individual in society, the life of societies in their time, the impact of ideas on daily experience—there is a whole other dimension of men and women that does not appear in his vision, or does so in a furtive way: the dimension that Georges Bataille has described better than anyone else. This is the world of unreason that underlies and sometimes blinds and kills reason; the world of the unconscious which, in ways that are always unverifiable and very difficult to detect, impregnates, directs, and sometimes enslaves consciousness; the world of those obscure instincts that, in unexpected ways, suddenly emerge to compete with ideas and often replace them as a form of action and can even destroy what these ideas have built up. Nothing could be further from the serene, harmonious, lucid, and healthy view of man held by Isaiah Berlin than this somber, confused, sickly, and fiery conception of Bataille. And yet I suspect that life is probably something that embraces and mixes these two enemies into a single truth, in all their powerful incongruity.

# 7

Truth, for Karl Popper, is not discovered: it is invented. It is, therefore, always a provisional truth, one that lasts only so long as it is not refuted. Truth is in the human mind, in imagination and reason, not hidden like a treasure in the nucleus of the atom or the abyss of space, waiting for a perceptive explorer to detect it or unearth and reveal it to the world, like a statue of an ancient goddess. Popper's truth is fragile, continually under the barrage of tests and experiments that seek to weigh it, measure it, try to undermine it—"falsify" it, according to his vocabulary—and substitute for it another truth, a process that has happened and will likely continue to happen in the course of that vast pilgrimage through time that we call progress or civilization.

Truth is, first, a hypothesis or a theory that attempts to solve a problem. Whether the result of laboratory experiments, the meditations of social reformers, or complicated mathematical calculations, it is presented to the world as objective knowledge of a specific aspect of reality. The hypothesis or theory is—ought to be—subject to the test of trial and error, where it can be verified or refuted by skeptical analysts. This is either an immediate or a protracted process, in the course of which the theory lives (but always under sentence of death) and operates, generates consequences, influences life, and causes changes—in medical treatment, in the armaments industry, in social organization, sexual behavior, or clothing styles—until all of a sudden another theory emerges, falsifying it, and what seemed firm collapses like a castle of cards in a gale. The new truth then takes the field, to undergo whatever tests and challenges the mind and science demand—that is, to live that hectic, dangerous existence proper to truth and knowledge in Popper's philosophy.

To be sure, no one has yet successfully refuted the contention that the world is round. But Popper advises us, against all objective evidence, to get used to thinking that the earth, in truth, only *seems* round, because in some way, at some time, the march of knowledge could also topple this truth, as it has already done with so many truths that seemed unshakable. But Popper's thinking is not relativistic or skeptically subjective. Truth has one foot firmly planted in objective reality, which he recognizes as existing independent from its influence on the human mind. This foot is—according to the definition of the Polish-American mathematician and philosopher Alfred Tarski, which Popper makes his own—the coincidence of the theory with the facts.

That truth has, or may have, a relative existence does not mean that truth *is* relative. While it lasts, until another falsifies it, truth is all-powerful. It is precarious only because all quests for knowledge are fallible, just as we humans are fallible. The possibility of error is always there, even behind what seems to us the most solid science. But this awareness of fallibility does not mean that truth is unattainable. It means that in order to reach the truth we must be tireless in our investigations, and prudent when we have arrived at certainties. We must be willing to revise and correct our own understanding, and be tolerant of people who challenge established verities.

That truth exists is demonstrated by the progress humanity has made in so many fields: in society and politics as well as in science and technology. By making mistakes, by learning from mistakes, humankind has come gradually to better understand nature and itself. This is an endless process in which we can move backward and sideways as well as forward. But even false hypotheses and theories may contain information that brings us closer to knowing the truth. Through mistakes eventually corrected, democratic culture has managed to guarantee citizens, in open societies, better material and cultural conditions and greater opportunities for deciding their own destiny. This is the "piecemeal approach" Popper espouses: a gradual or reformist approach, the opposite of "revolution" or making a *tabula rasa* of everything extant.

Although for Popper truth is always suspect (as in the wonderful title of the drama *La verdad sospechosa* [*Suspect Truth*] by Spain's Golden Age playwright Juan Ruiz de Alarcón), during its reign, human life is tamely organized as a function of that truth and, because of it, undergoes modifications that are both minute and transcendent. What matters, for progress to be possible, for knowledge to be enriched rather than impoverished, is that the reigning truths must always be subject to criticism, exposed to tests, verifications, and challenges that confirm or replace them with truths that are closer to that definitive and total truth (surely unattainable and perhaps nonexistent) whose lure has piqued humans' curiosity and appetite to know ever since reason displaced superstition as a source of knowledge.

So Popper makes criticism—that is, the exercise of freedom—the foundation of progress. Without criticism, without the possibility of falsifying all the certainties, there can be no advances in scientific understanding or improvements in social life. If truth, if all truths, are not subject to the test of trial and error, if there is no freedom for people to question and compare the validity of all the theories that claim to answer their questions, the production of knowledge becomes shackled and knowledge itself can be perverted. Then—instead of rational truths—myths, acts of faith, and magic hold sway. The kingdom of the irrational, of dogma and taboo, regains its domain, as in bygone days, when people were not yet rational and free individuals but were part of an enslaved mass, just part of the tribe.

This irrationality can take a religious form, as in fundamentalist societies, where no one can impugn or contradict the sacred truths, or it can take a secular form, as in totalitarian societies where the official truth is protected from free examination in the name of a "scientific doctrine" such as Marxism-Leninism. In both cases, however, a voluntary or forced abdication of the right to criticize causes rationality to deteriorate, culture to become impoverished, and science to devolve into mystification and bewitchment. Beneath the jacket and tie of civilized men, human-

ity reverts to the loincloth and magical consciousness of the savage.

We have no other way to progress toward truth
other than to trip, fall, and stand up, time and again.
Error will always be there because the right thing
is, to some extent, complicit with it. As we undertake the great challenge of distinguishing truth from
lies—a goal that is quite possible to achieve—we must
keep in mind that in this task there are never any
definitive achievements which cannot later be challenged, and no knowledge which cannot be revisited
and revised. In the great forest of misperceptions and
deceptions through which humankind roams, truth
can clear a way only through rational and systematic criticism of what passes for knowledge. Without
this privileged expression of freedom—the right to
criticize—we are condemned to oppression, brutality, and obscurantism. Probably no thinker has made
freedom so essential a condition for humanity as Karl
Popper. For him, freedom does more than guarantee
civilized forms of existence and stimulate cultural
creativity; it is something much more distinctive and
radical. Critical thinking is the basic requirement for
knowing. It allows humanity to learn from its own
errors and overcome them.

Popper's theory of knowledge is the best philosophical justification for the ethical value that most

characterizes democratic culture: tolerance. If there are no absolute and eternal truths, if the only way for knowledge to progress is by making and correcting mistakes, we should all recognize that our own truths may not be right and that what looks to us like our adversaries' errors may in fact be correct. To recognize that margin of error in ourselves and of correctness in others is to believe that through entering into dialogue and peaceful coexistence it is much easier to identify error and truth than through the imposition of a single, official way of thinking to which all must subscribe for fear of being punished, disgraced, or destroyed.

At the dawn of human history there was only the tribe, the closed society. The sovereign individual, freed from that body that jealously closed upon itself in order to defend its members from animals, lightning bolts, evil spirits, and other innumerable fears of the primitive world, is a late creation of humanity. It arrives with the appearance of the critical spirit: with the discovery that life's problems can be solved by individual members of society, when they obtain the right to exercise rationality independent of religious and political authorities.

According to Popper's theory, this frontier moment of civilization—the passage from a closed to an open society—began in Greece, with the pre-Socratics (Thales, Anaximander, Anaximenes), and achieved its decisive impulse with Socrates. Popper's formulation has been the object of endless controversy; but putting dates and names aside, the substantive part of his thesis remains persuasive. At some moment, by accident or as the consequence of a complex process, knowing, for certain people, ceased to be magical and superstitious, a body of sacred beliefs protected by taboo. A critical spirit emerged that subjected religious truths—the only ones in force until then—to the scalpel of rational analysis and to collation with practical experience. This transformation led to the prodigious flowering of science, the arts, and technology, of human creativity in general, and, in like fashion, the birth of the singular, decollectivized individual, and the foundation of a culture of freedom. For better or for worse (since there is no way to prove that this move has maximized human happiness), the detribalization of intellectual life would accelerate and propel certain societies toward systematic growth in every domain.

Within the almost infinite series of nomenclatures and classifications that the wise and the mad have proposed to describe reality, Popper's is one of the most transparent. In his scheme, reality comprises three "worlds." The first world consists of natural and material objects; the second world is the subjective and private world of the individual mind; the third world is the domain of cultural creativity. The second world encompasses the private subjectivity of each individual, his nontransferable ideas, images, sensations, and feelings. The creations of the third world, although born in the individual's subjectivity, become public goods: they are the scientific theories, juridical institutions, ethical principles, and works of art that make up our entire cultural heritage.

In civilization's most primitive stage, Popper's first world probably regulated existence. Early societies organized themselves in response to brute force or the rigors of nature—a drought, the lion's claws—against which humankind was often powerless. In a tribal, animistic, magical society, the boundary between the second and third worlds must have been very tenuous and continually dissolving, as the chieftain or religious authority (almost always the same person) imposed its own subjectivity on other members of the group, and subjects relinquished theirs. The third world remained almost stationary; the life of the tribe went on within a strict routine of rules and beliefs that ensured the continuity and repetition of what was already established. Its main feature was terror in the face of change. Any innovation must have been perceived as a threat, presaging an invasion of external forces that could only lead to the annihilation of the social structure to which frightened and forlorn individuals must cling. Enslaved and not responsible for his own fate, each tribal member was a mere part, irreparably linked to other parts, within a social mechanism that preserved and defended itself against the enemies and dangers that lurked outside the fortress of tribal life.

In Popper's view, the birth of a critical spirit broke down the walls of this closed society and exposed humanity to an unknown experience: individual responsibility. No longer the submissive subject, adhering without question to the complex system of prohibitions and rules that governed social life, the individual became a citizen who judged and analyzed for himself and eventually rebelled against what seemed absurd, false, or abusive. This freedom to criticize placed a heavy load on the shoulders of human beings. Now they must decide for themselves, unaided, what was beneficial and what harmful, how to confront life's countless challenges, whether society was functioning as it should or whether it needed to be changed.

This burden proved too heavy for many. And for that reason, says Popper, at the very dawn of the open society—when the individual became the protagonist of history—a contrary impulse was also born, an impulse to impede and negate the individ-

ual and to resuscitate or preserve that old tribal society in which the human being was a bee within its
hive, relieved of responsibility for making individual
decisions, for confronting the unknown, for resolv-
ing at its own risk the infinite problems of a universe
free of the gods and demons of idolatry and magic.
This contrary impulse remains to this day a constant
challenge to the reason of sovereign individuals.

At the mysterious moment when the critical spirit
was born, humanity changed course. Popper's third
world, populated with the creations of a spiritual energy unencumbered by restrictions or censorship, began to prosper and proliferate and to exercise more
and more influence over the first and second worlds—
over nature, social interactions, and the interior life
of individuals. Ideas, scientific truths, and rationality
beat back brute force, religious dogma, superstition,
and irrational fears as the guiding principles of society, though not without reversals, standstills, and de-
tours that returned humankind to its point of departure. From this struggle grew a democratic culture,
made of sovereign individuals equal before the law,
and an open society where they were free to follow
the dictates of their own mind. The long and difficult
advance of freedom through history would lead the
West to develop medicines that could halt epidem-
ics and spacecraft that could travel beyond earth's atmosphere, but also chemical, atomic, and biological

weapons capable of destroying populations and reducing the planet to rubble in an instant.

The fear of change, of the unknown, of the unlimited responsibilities that are a consequence of the critical spirit has allowed closed societies, adopting diverse guises, to survive until our day and, at many moments in history, to hold sway over open societies. The battle is not won, nor, probably, will it ever be. The "call of the tribe"—of that form of existence in which individuals enslave themselves to a religion or doctrine or chieftain who assumes responsibility for answering all of life's questions—evidently touches a chord deep in the human heart. For this call is heard time after time by nations and peoples and, even within open societies, by individuals and collectivities that struggle tirelessly to negate the culture of freedom. And counter to what one might believe, those who maintain the most implacable opposition to an open society are often among its most direct beneficiaries. Ironically, they exercise their freedom of speech, thought, and movement to advocate a return to a magical, primitive world, preferring to be instruments of blind and impersonal forces that direct the march of history.

In his luminous book *The Open Society and Its Enemies,* Popper expounded another thesis that has been widely questioned. He claimed that the greatest philosopher of his time (and perhaps of all time) was Plato, the first in a long line of totalitarian philosophers who—via Comte and Hegel—would reach their apogee in Karl Marx. Nuances aside, Popper's thinking on the subject of totalitarian philosophers hit the mark, because it allowed him to identify one of the most sinuous and effective enemies of the culture of freedom: he called it "historicism."

Those who think that the history of humanity is "written" before it happens, that it is the performance of a preexistent libretto, fashioned by God, by nature, by the development of reason, or by class struggle and the means of production; who believe that life is a force or a social and economic mechanism that particular individuals have little or no power to alter; who think this movement of humanity through time is rational, coherent, and therefore predictable; who, in short, think history makes some secret sense, that, despite its infinite episodic diversity, gives to everything a coordinated logic and orders it like a puzzle, with each piece finding its proper place— these people are, according to Popper, "historicists."

No matter whether they are Platonic, Hegelian, Comtian, or Marxist, or—at the other extreme—followers of Machiavelli, Vico, Spengler, or Toynbee, historicists are consciously or unconsciously frightened of freedom and secretly afraid of the responsibility that comes from conceiving of life as an un-ending creation, a malleable lump of clay that each society, culture, and generation molds however it wishes. Historicists do not want to assume the direc-tor's role, accepting full credit for what, in each case, humankind achieves or loses.

As Popper points out, history has no order, logic, or sense, much less a rational direction that soci-ologists, economists, or ideologues can detect in ad-vance, "scientifically." History is organized by histo-rians; they are the ones who make it coherent and intelligible, through the use of points of view and interpretations that are, always, partial, provisional, and, in the final analysis, as subjective as artistic con-structs. Those who believe that one of the functions of the social sciences is to "foresee" the future, to "predict" history, are victims of an illusion, for that is an unattainable goal.

What, then, is history? A constant improvisation, a lively chaos to which historians give an appearance of order, an almost infinite contradictory multiplica-tion of events that—to help us understand them—the social sciences reduce to arbitrary schemes and to syntheses and charts which are inevitably a pale replica and even a caricature of real history, that ver-tiginous totality of human activity which always overflows rational and intellectual attempts at comprehension. Popper does not reject history books, nor does he deny that knowledge of the past can enrich humankind and help it to better confront the future. He merely asks us to take into account the fact that all written histories are partial and arbitrary, that they reflect barely an atom of the unfinished social universe in which human beings reside—a "whole" always in the process of making and remaking itself, unexhausted by political, economic, cultural, institutional, religious histories.

What we normally understand by history, Popper says in *The Open Society,* is generally the history of power politics, which is nothing but "the history of international crime and mass murder (including, it is true, some of the attempts to suppress them)." This understanding of history is "an offence against every decent conception of mankind." The history of the conquests, crimes, and other acts of violence perpetrated by bosses and despots whom books have transformed into heroes can give only a pale idea of the integral experience of all those who suffered their brutality or enjoyed their stories. And it reveals little of the effects and reverberations that the actions of every culture, society, and civilization have had on others, both their contemporaries and those that followed them. If the history of humanity is a vast current of development and progress with abundant meanderings, regressions, and full stops (a thesis Popper does not negate), it cannot be contained in its infinite diversity and complexity within the walls of a historical discipline.

Those who have tried to uncover, in the unencompassable disorder, certain laws to which this human development is tied have perpetrated what for Popper is perhaps the gravest crime a politician or intellectual can commit (but not an artist, for whom this is a legitimate right): creating an "unreal construct," an artificial entelechy that aspires to represent itself as scientific truth when it is nothing but an act of faith, a metaphysical or magical proposal. Naturally, not all historicist theories are equivalent; some, like Marx's, have greater subtlety and gravity than, say, that of an Arnold Toynbee, who reduced the history of humanity to twenty-one civilizations, no more, no less.

The future cannot be forecast. The evolution of humankind in the past does not allow us to deduce any direction in human activity. Not only in historical terms but also from a logical point of view, prediction would be an absurd pretension, for without a doubt the growth of knowledge influences history. And we have no way to predict, by rational means, the evolution of knowledge. It is not possible, therefore, to anticipate a future course that will be, in good measure, determined by technical and scientific discoveries and inventions that we cannot know in advance.

International events provide a good argument in support of the unforeseeability of history. Who would have anticipated the decline of communism in the world, or the sharp rise of religious fundamentalisms? And who could have imagined the global role that new media would play in both evading censorship and disseminating hatred? But the fact that historical laws do not exist does not mean that certain patterns in human evolution cannot be detected. And the fact that one cannot predict the future does not mean that all social forecasting is impossible. Within specific fields, the social sciences can establish that, under certain conditions, certain facts will most likely occur: the indiscriminate issuing of currency will almost always bring about inflation, for example. And there is no doubt that in certain arenas, like the sciences, international law, and individual freedom, one can trace a more or less clear line of progress up to the present. But it would be imprudent to assume, even in these domains, that a past record of advances guarantees irreversible progress in the future.

Humanity can regress and fall, nullifying its past achievements. Never have collective killings reached the magnitude of those produced in the twentieth century by two world wars. The Jewish Holocaust perpetrated by the Nazis and the extermination of millions of dissidents by Soviet communists are ample proof that barbarism can blossom anew with unwonted force in societies which seem to have attained a high level of civilization. The growth of Islamic fundamentalism in states like Iran proves the ease with which history can follow trajectories that regress rather than advance with respect to individual liberty.

But even if the historian's function is to relate singular and specific events and not to uncover laws or generalizations regarding human activity, one cannot write or understand history without a point of view, that is, without a perspective or an interpretation. The historicist's error, says Popper, lies in confusing a "historical interpretation" with a theory or law. Interpretation is partial and, within that limitation, it can be useful for ordering, partially, what otherwise would be a chaotic accumulation of events. Interpreting history as the result of a class or race struggle, or of religious ideas, or of a conflict between an open society and a closed one, can be illustrative, so long as we do not attribute universal and exclusive validity to any of these interpretations. History admits many coincidental, complementary, or contradictory interpretations, but no law in the sense of a unique and inevitable course of events.

What invalidates the interpretations of the historicists is that they give interpretations the status of laws to which human events must yield docilely, as objects submit to the law of gravity and the tides to the movement of the moon. In this sense, there are no laws in history, because history is, for better or for worse (Popper and many of us believe the first), "free," a child born of the freedom of humankind and therefore uncontrollable, yet capable of the most surprising and extraordinary occurrences. Of course an acute observer will notice certain tendencies in history, but these assume a multitude of specific and variable conditions. When historicists talk of "tendencies," they tend to omit those local, temporal conditions and stretch tendencies into general laws. By proceeding in this way, they denaturalize reality and present an abstract model of history that does not reflect collective life in its temporal unfolding but, if anything, reveals their own inventiveness—or ingenuity—and also their secret fear of the unforeseeable. "It really looks," says the final paragraph of *The Poverty of Historicism,* "as if the historicists were trying to compensate themselves for the loss of an unchanging world by clinging to the belief that change can be foreseen because it is ruled by an unchanging law."

Popper's concept of written history resembles, exactly, what I have always believed the novel to be:

an arbitrary organization of human reality that protects humankind against the anguish produced by our intuition of the world, of life, as a vast disorder. To have the power to persuade, all novels ought to impose themselves on the reader's consciousness as a convincing order, an organized and intelligible world whose parts dovetail within a harmonic system, a "whole" that relates and sublimates them. What we call the genius of Tolstoy, of Henry James, of Proust, of Faulkner has to do not only with the vigor of their characters, their questioning psychology, the subtle or labyrinthine prose, the powerful imagination, but, also, most significantly, with the architectural coherence of their fictitious worlds, their solidity, their seamlessness. That rigorous and intelligent order, where nothing is gratuitous or incomprehensible, where life flows in a logical and inevitable channel, seduces us because it calms us: unconsciously we superimpose it onto the real world and the real world, then, fleetingly ceases to be what it is—vertigo, pandemonium, immeasurable absurdity, bottomless chaos, multiple disorder—and gains coherence. Rationalizing and ordering our surroundings, the novel restores that confidence which human beings are loathe to give up of knowing what we are, where we are, and—above all—where we are going.

It is no coincidence that often the best novels are

written during times that precede the great convulsions of history. The most fertile moments for fiction are those when collective certainties—religious or political faith, social and ideological consensus—break down, for it is then that ordinary people sense they lack solid ground beneath their feet, and look to the order and coherence of the fictional world for a mantle over that great insecurity and confusion of unknowns that life has become. It is not a coincidence that societies living through marked periods of social, institutional, and moral disintegration often generate the most rigorous narratives, the best organized, most logical "orders"—those of Sade and Kafka, Proust and Joyce, Dostoyevsky and Tolstoy. Fictional constructs that radically employ free will and acts of disobedience against the limits imposed by the human condition—a symbolic deicide—are secret testimonies to a panicked fear that the fate of humankind is a "fear of freedom." This radicalism can be found in works like Herodotus's *The Nine Books of History,* Michelet's *History of the French Revolution,* or Gibbon's *The Decline and Fall of the Roman Empire,* all prodigies of erudition, ambition, good prose, and fantasy. But these works also represent the daunting intellectual creations with which, at different times, in different ways, we have tried to deny that very suspicion. Fortunately, a deep-seated fear of freedom has not only engendered tyrants, totalitarian philosophers, dogmatic religions, and historicism; it has also produced some great novels.

What Popper suggests as an alternative to "historicism" is "piecemeal engineering," or the gradual reform of society. He argues in *The Poverty of Historicism* that once we realize we can improve things only "a bit," then we must also realize that we can make these improvements only "bit by bit"—by continually readjusting the parts, instead of undertaking a total reconstruction of society. Proceeding in this way has the advantage that at each stage we can evaluate the result achieved and learn from our errors. The "revolutionary" method—which is historicist and holistic—closes off this possibility because by showing contempt for the particular and becoming obsessively fixated on the whole, it very quickly moves away from concrete experience. It becomes an abstract model, detached from reality and alien to experience. In its desire to match up to social reality, it ends up sacrificing everything else: reason, freedom, and, at times, common sense.

In Popper's view, any notion of planning is historicist through and through. Planning supposes that history cannot just be predicted but also directed and organized, like a work of engineering. This utopia is dangerous, because therein lurks the threat of totalitarianism. There is no way to centralize all the forms of knowledge contained in all the individual minds that make up a society, or of ascertaining the desires, ambitions, needs, and interests that will together determine the historical development of a country. Planning, taken to its logical conclusion, leads to the centralization of power. It progressively dominates the development of all the disparate forces and aspects of social life, and it imposes an authoritarian control over the behavior of institutions and individuals. Planning, defined as the controlled and scientific ordering of social evolution, is a pipe dream. Whenever it is imposed, it leads to the destruction of freedom, to totalitarian regimes in which central powers, under the pretext of "rationalizing" limited resources in an efficient manner, take upon themselves the right to deny citizens any initiative or diversity and force them to behave in certain ways.

Of course in many free societies there are planning departments that do not curtail public freedoms. But these departments "plan" in a very relative or symbolic way. They usually just give information and advice about economic activity, without compulsively imposing policies or goals. This is not, in a strict sense, planning but rather investigating and advising—activities that are perfectly compatible with the functioning of a competitive market and a democratic society. Unlike the "utopian or holistic engineer"—the revolutionary—Popper's "piecemeal engineer" is a reformist who admits that he or she cannot know "everything" and that there is no way to predict or control the movements of free society. The piecemeal engineer puts the part before the whole, the present before the future, and the problems and needs of men and women in the here and now before that uncertain mirage that we may think of as our destiny.

Reformists do not claim to change everything or to act according to some remote, global design. Instead, they try to change concrete conditions in the present, and they look to solve problems in such a way that partial but effective and constant progress can be made. They know that it is only by continually working on the parts that the social whole can be improved. They look to reduce or abolish poverty, unemployment, and discrimination, suggesting new ways of improving living conditions, and they are always sensitive to the complex diversity of contradictory interests and aspirations, seeking that necessary balance between them so as to minimize injustice and create new opportunities. Reformists do not seek to bring happiness to men and women because they know that this is a matter for individuals and not for the state. Their aims are less ambitious and more realistic: to reduce injustice and seek to rectify the social and economic causes of individual suffering.

Why do reformists prefer to modify or reform existing institutions instead of replacing them, as revolutionaries try to do? Because, as Popper says in one of the most free-ranging essays in his book *Conjectures and Refutations: The Growth of Scientific Knowledge*, the way that institutions function does not depend just on how they are composed—their structure, rules, the responsibilities assigned to them, or to the people in charge of them—but also on the traditions and customs of the larger society. The most important of these traditions is the culture's "moral framework," the sense of justice and social sensibility that a culture has developed throughout its history. One cannot erase this. The delicate, deeply rooted psychology and mood of a society cannot be abolished or abruptly replaced, as revolutionaries might wish. For, in the final instance, it is the way that institutions resonate with this mood and psychological outlook that determines whether or not they are successful. However well thought out institutions may be, they will achieve their aims only if they are attuned to that indescribable, unwritten moral context that is so decisive in the life of a nation. This constant adjustment of institutions to the traditions and ethics of the larger society, which develop and change much more slowly than institutions, is only possible through "piecemeal engineering," whose gradual course corrections can prevent errors from becoming embedded (something that a "holistic" or utopian methodology cannot do).

Reformism is compatible with freedom—or rather, it depends on freedom—because critical analysis is at the heart of its enterprise. With its critical approach, reformism can always keep a balance between the individual and power, and prevent the individual from being crushed. By contrast, utopian or holistic engineering will lead, sooner or later to the accumulation of power and the suppression of criticism (that is, to dictatorship). And the route to this eventual outcome—even though we might be oblivious to it at the time—is through controls, which are, of necessity, a part of any regime that tries to plan social development. Economic and other cultural controls stifle initiative and freedom and eventually undermine individual sovereignty, turning citizens into puppets. There are, of course, a great variety of intermediate stages between a regulated democracy and a totalitarian or police state. But, according to Popper, while in the freest society some form of power must place certain limits and conditions on individual behavior—for without them, society would slide into anarchy—it is also true that any forms of control must be constantly monitored and balanced, because they always contain the seeds of authoritarianism, the beginnings of a threat against individual freedom.

The state, says Popper, is a "necessary evil." Without it, there would be no coexistence or any equitable redistribution of wealth; freedom, left to its own devices, is a source of enormous imbalances and inequalities that themselves often lead to abuse of power. Without a state, there would be no way to correct these abuses among individuals. But the state is evil in the sense that its existence places in all instances, even in the freest democracies, significant limitations on individual sovereignty. The state poses a constant threat that its growth might undermine the fragile foundation of freedom on which, through history, men and women have built that most mysterious and beautiful human creation: the culture of freedom.

From his very first book, Popper was opposed to a fashion that, at the time, did not yet exist: the fashion for linguistic distraction. Much of contemporary Western thought after the Second World War would become obsessively preoccupied with the limitations and power of language, to such an extent that at a certain moment—in the 1960s—one had the impression that all the human sciences, from philosophy to history, including anthropology and politics, were becoming branches of linguistics. And this formal perspective—words organized among themselves, dissociated from their referent, the objective world, from life as lived—which was being deployed in every discipline, would end up turning Western culture into a kind of protoplasmic philological, semiological, or grammatical speculation. It became a great rhetorical fireworks display in which ideas and concerns about the "big issues" more or less disappeared, banished by the exclusive preoccupation with expression itself, with the formal structures of each and every science and form of knowledge.

Popper never took this path, and this doubtlessly explains, in part, why throughout his long intellectual career he was never a fashionable philosopher and why his ideas would remain confined for a long time to academic circles. For him, language "communicates" things outside itself, and one must try to use it functionally. To become distracted by exploring language for its own sake, as something dissociated from content, which is the reality that words have a duty to express, is not just a waste of time, in his view, but also frivolous, a distraction from what is essential, which is the search for truth. And for Popper, truth is always *outside* words, something that words can communicate but never ever produce by themselves.

He argued in *Objective Knowledge* that simplicity and lucidity was the moral duty of every intellectual, that lack of clarity was a "sin" and pretentiousness a "crime." Simplicity, for Popper, means using language in such a way that words are not very important in their own right: they are transparent and allow ideas to be expressed without embellishment. As he put it in *The Open Society*, "Our 'operational definitions' have the advantage of helping us to shift the problem into a field in which nothing or little depends on words. Clear speaking is speaking in such a way that words do not matter." This is one of the most direct statements I have found anywhere that challenges the reigning orthodoxy of modern Western culture that orders us to mistrust words, since they can play the cruelest tricks on anyone not using them wisely or not paying them sufficient attention.

Yet Popper did not perhaps pay sufficient attention to the expressive forms of language. He was right to believe that language should not be an end in itself or even a dominant preoccupation, for it might profoundly distort the content of knowledge. The supposed identity between form and content does not exist even where it might seem inevitable, in literature, because, as Gabriel Ferrater once said in a famous *boutade,* one cannot confuse Dante's *terza rima* with the torments of hell. This belief guarded Popper against a temptation to which many famous intellectuals of his day succumbed: of pushing the "big issues" into the background and concentrating instead on marginal topics having to do with the formal expression of a science or philosophy. Like the great classic works of philosophy, Popper's thought has always dealt with fundamental concerns, large questions, truth and lies, objective and magical or religious knowledge, freedom and tyranny, the individual and the state, superstition and science. But without a doubt his thought has been affected by his underestimation of the power of words, the rash supposition that one can use them as if they have no life of their own.

Words are always important. If one undervalues them, they take their revenge, introducing ambiguity, double or treble meanings, into a text that seeks to be aseptic and unequivocal. Popper's reluctance to consider language as an autonomous reality, with its own impulses and tendencies, has had a negative effect on his writing, which at times can be imprecise and confusing. His use of terms and classifications is not always successful because they are easily misunderstood. To use the term "historicism" for a totalitarian view of history or mere ideology is questionable because it suggests a challenge to history itself, which is far from Popper's philosophy. His use of terms such as "piecemeal engineering" and "utopian or holistic engineering" is even more suspect because much simpler phrases are available, such as "reformism" and "radicalism" or a "liberal approach" versus a "totalitarian approach." Hayek, for example, criticized Popper's use of the word "engineer" for a social reformer because of the unconscious association with Stalinist vocabulary, which defined writers as "engineers of souls." And there is an internal contradiction in Popper's calling social reformers "engineers," since he so persuasively argued against the idea of planning—the illusion that one can organize society from a position of centralized power.

It is good that philosophers or scientists do not restrict themselves merely to analyzing the language that they use, because this can be a rather sterile, and byzantine, intellectual pursuit. But it is essential for thinkers to pay due attention to the way they express themselves so that they are in control of the words in their texts and not the passive servants of language. Popper's work, which ranks among the most suggestive and innovative of our time, has this blemish: his words, so disdained by him, sometimes tangle and distort his ideas rather than disciplining them. They do not do justice to the depth and originality of his thought.

Roland Barthes, whose ideas on language are dia-
metrically opposed to Popper's, wrote in *Leçon*: "In
the order of knowledge, for things to become what
they are, what they have been, one needs the following ingredient: the spice of words. It is the flavour
of words that makes this knowledge profound and
rich." In Popper's functional language, words have
no spice. They lack that balance between content
and expression that he sought in his ideal of a "simple and lucid" language. In his books, even in those
where the wisdom of his analysis is most evident,
the complexity of a thought never comes through
to us in its true splendor but arrives watered down
or muddied by his writing. Unlike Ortega y Gasset,
whose style improved his ideas, shaping them with
nuance and depth, Popper's opaque prose meanders
across the shallow surface of his thought.

Putting Roland Barthes alongside Popper is not
completely arbitrary. On the question of language,
they represent two poles of excess. Unlike Popper,
who thought that language did not matter, Barthes
thought, in the final analysis, that language alone
was important, since it is the center of power, of *all*
power. An essayist of immense talent but also frivolous and self-regarding, who showed off and then
vanished behind all those words—discourse, text,
*langue, parole,* and so on—which he described with
such brilliance and sophistry, Barthes ended up "dem-

onstrating" that it was not men and women who spoke but rather language which spoke through them, molding them through a sinuous and invisible dictatorship: "Language . . . is neither reactionary nor progressive; it is quite simply fascist, because fascism is not about preventing speech, it is about compelling people to speak" (*Leçon,* p. 14). Only literary works that break with the dominant language can escape this dictatorship, but their escape is temporary since they will in turn become the dominant language.

Freedom, for Barthes, can exist only outside of language. (Presumably, therefore the freest men and women would be autistic or deaf and dumb?). When one condenses Barthes' thought, removing it from the elegant texts he wrote, then one can see very clearly how superficial, provocative, playful, humorous, light, and often vacuous it is. But when one has to deal with this thought in the original texts, embellished by the elegance of the prose, the control of nuance, the enchanting subtlety of the phrase, it seems deep, it seems to express some transcendent truth. Nothing of the sort: it is just a beautiful rhetorical mirage.

It is simply not true that language is the seat of all power. What a sophism! The elegant prose that Barthes wrote, his iridescent style, gave his ephem-

eral ideas the appearance of penetration and permanence, while Popper's ambitious and profound system of thought has been undermined by a linguistic
style that could never support the ideas he attempted
to express. Although ideas are not made up just of
words, as Barthes believed, without the appropriate
words to communicate them, ideas can never be all
that they might be.

As a young man in his native Austria, Karl Popper
(born in 1902) was a Marxist. Then, disillusioned by
Marxism, he became a social democrat for some
years. He left the social democratic movement when
it embraced statist and collectivist tendencies. But
Popper's thought was not at odds with modern social democracy once he stripped it of its socialist illusions and its Marxist "historicism." On the other
hand, conservatives can also claim Popper as one of
their own because his "piecemeal approach"—the continuous, systematic, reform of society—resonates
with their desire to reconcile tradition and modernity and to achieve a harmonious, nontraumatic evolution of society. His body of thought is so rich that
it can feed all these different currents of democratic
culture.

But without doubt, the definition that fits Popper
best is that of a classic liberal, a philosopher in the

great tradition of Adam Smith, John Stuart Mill, Benjamin Constant, and Alexis de Tocqueville. They produced a body of work that established the intellectual foundations of political modernity, first in Europe and then in the rest of the world. However, to use the word "liberal" today is to commit the sin that Popper tried at all costs to avoid. For in contemporary political usage, "liberal" lacks clarity and can mean many different, and contradictory, things. In Great Britain and the United States, for example, the term refers to progressives who align with social democratic and even socialist positions. In France, Italy, Spain, and Latin America, the difference between a liberal and a conservative is very difficult to see, because many parties and politicians who call themselves "liberals" defend the status quo—those hybrid regimes with their interventionist markets, monopolistic practices, and economic nationalism which are the very antithesis of what classic liberalism, in the tradition of Adam Smith, propounds.

Popper, along with Hayek and van Mises, is one of the great pioneers of classical liberalism, after a long period in which liberal ideas and policies suffered serious setbacks. This hiatus was due not only to the development of fascist and Marxist totalitarianism but also to the espousal in Western social democracies of what Hayek would call the "constructivist fallacy": the idea that large social institutions can be redesigned in a rational way to better accomplish their aims. This notion is at the root of such "planning" regimes as Keynesian economic policies, the New Deal, and contemporary populist ideologies through which the state's influence in economic and social life increased in size and power. Then came the counteroffensive, headed by Reagan in the United States and Thatcher in the United Kingdom, which favored the competitive market. Dubbed "neo-conservatism" in the United States, it purported to represent a return to classic liberalism.

The two seminal books in the resurrection of classic liberalism, *The Road to Serfdom* (1944) by Hayek and *The Open Society and Its Enemies* (1945), by Popper, were published at almost the same time. They passed unnoticed by the general public and were scorned by an intellectual and political establishment that favored economic nationalism and Keynesian ideas of state intervention in citizens' welfare—the charitable state—or else openly supported socialist ideas of centralized and planned economies. Yet the ideas expounded by Hayek, Popper, and von Mises—and later developed (often from a critical perspective) by people such as Milton Friedman and his Chicago school of economics, or James Buchanan and his school of public choice, or the American philosopher

Robert Nozick—would keep liberal doctrine alive and in a state of renewal as an alternative to socialism and mercantilist capitalism.

After the end of the 1980s, with the fall of collectivist regimes in Central Europe and the accelerated liberalization of social democratic regimes, liberalism, in its different forms, achieved a new prominence. Thanks to it, Western countries and those that copied the West's economic model—Japan and other countries of the Pacific Rim, especially China—realized unprecedented prosperity and material development. And with the end of the cold war and the disintegration of the Soviet bloc, it seemed that we had embarked on an era of peace and prosperity, in which nations could concentrate less on arming themselves and more on protecting the environment, strengthening democracy, supporting culture, and developing science and technology "for peace."

The surprises that history has dealt us in recent years warn us to be prudent and not to embrace the optimism of those like Francis Fukuyama who once believed—but no longer—that we had reached a Hegelian end of history, with the triumph of liberalism in the world. Such a victory, as we have seen, is far from certain. In the so-called Third World, the old barbarism persists and looks as if it will continue for some time yet, with exceptions that can be counted on the fingers of one hand. And although the collapse of the communist regimes of Central Europe was an extraordinary event in the cause of freedom, there is no guarantee, in these countries, that a liberal system will triumph. In many of them, as in the Soviet Union itself, we can see emerging from the rubble of communism some sinister demons of the past—extreme chauvinist nationalism, anti-Semitism, religious fundamentalism, and the like.

Furthermore, perhaps the one unshakable principle of liberal doctrine is that it cannot achieve any final victory. For liberalism, there can only be partial and fleeting victories, with the constant threat of stumbles and reversals. If history is not written in advance, then anything can happen—we can move forward or backward. Progress exists, but society might achieve it in a convoluted way. One generation might go back on what it took two generations to achieve. The measure of progress is not economic development—that is a consequence—but rather the advance of freedom in every sphere: economic, political, cultural, institutional, and ethical. And it is very far from being the case that those societies which have, through economic freedom, raised production and improved living standards have, in the same way, at the same pace, improved freedom in other areas of social life.

The battle for freedom is ongoing and is fought

on many fronts. In liberal terms—terms much broader than any political party that might seek to monopolize them—this means the defense of the individual, civil society, private property, gradual progress through reforms, political, religious, and cultural tolerance, government limited by the rule of law, an efficient, honest judicial system independent of political power, and a market economy with stable and fair laws that respects the state but cannot be manipulated by it, or by private interests.

This range of liberal principles inevitably becomes more nuanced when put into practice. That is why the liberal option has progressed in certain countries governed by socialist or conservative parties, while it has suffered setbacks as a result of policies imposed by governments that call themselves liberal. What is important is the content, not the label attached to it. Everything that works toward the decentralization of power—the breaking up of central power into many specific loci of power—is good for the cause of liberty. As is the spread of private property among citizens through goods or shares, the creation of competitive markets in place of monopolies, and the transfer to civil society of businesses and powers that once belonged to the state.

But none of these moves can truly advance the cause of freedom if society merely reduces the role of the state and promotes individual initiative and competence. It must also foster the development of a critical spirit without which citizens cannot really benefit from the rights and powers that liberal society bestows upon them. Paradoxically, the progress of liberal economic policies that we have seen in Western countries in recent decades has not contributed in any significant way to the development of alert, inquiring, critical citizens who are aware that they must play a leading role in freeing themselves from state paternalism and become actively involved in civic life and social action. Quite the reverse. The norm has been the dulling of any sense of civic responsibility, the increasing indifference of young people toward public life, and the almost complete abdication of civil society in favor of a small political class when it comes to matters of great social importance.

Material progress and the consolidation of liberal democracy in Western societies have lead to a widespread conformism at best, if not an attitude of repugnance and contempt for politics and public life. And meanwhile, cultural life has been hampered, tamed, and corrupted by the massive invasion of semi- or pseudo-cultural products, disseminated by the mass media, that dull our imagination, our creative spirit, and our critical intelligence.

Is it not here that we find confirmation of Popper's theory that freedom can be threatened at the very core of what seems to be its strongest bastion? In the immediate future, the challenges to freedom in democratic societies will probably not come from totalitarian ideologies, which are already in an advanced state of decline, but rather from more surreptitious enemies, which are more difficult to overcome. I am not speaking now of terrorist cells or insurgencies, but of boredom, tedium, cultural and spiritual anomie, triviality, conformism, and the comfortable routines that only the beneficiaries of freedom enjoy.

## Bibliography

Barthes, Roland. *Leçon*. Paris: Seuil, 1978.

Gibbon, Edward. *The Decline and Fall of the Roman Empire*. 8 vols. New York: Modern Library, 1932.

Herodotus. *The Histories*. Tr. and intro. by Aubrey de Selincourt. 9 vols. Baltimore: Penguin, 1961.

Michelet, Jules. *History of the French Revolution*. Tr. Charles Cocks. Ed. And intro. Gordon Wright. 7 vols. Chicago and London: University of Chicago Press, 1967.

Popper, Karl R. *The Open Society and Its Enemies*. 2 vols. London: Routledge, 1945.

—— *The Poverty of Historicism*. 1957. London: Routledge & Kegan Paul, 1960.

Ruiz de Alarcón y Mendoza, Juan. *La Verdad Sospechosa y Los Pechos Privilegiados*. 8th. ed. Madrid: Espasa-Calpe, 1962.

## ACKNOWLEDGMENTS

Chapters 1, 2, and 3 are based on public lectures delivered at Emory University in Atlanta as the 2006 Richard Ellmann Lectures in Modern Literature. I wish to thank Professor Ronald Schuchard for his cordial invitation to participate, and the Emory community for their hospitality and interest in my work. I am also indebted to Professors Robert Crawford of the University of St. Andrews, Marjorie Howes of Boston University, and Edward Mendelson of Columbia University for joining in many lively conversations and offering public comments as the lectures unfolded. Chapter 4 draws on two additional lectures: "The Challenge of Nationalism," delivered in London in 1998, and a portion of "The Elephant and Culture," delivered in Lima in 1981. For her translation of Chapters 1, 3, and 4 I wish to extend my thanks to Kristin Keenan de Cueto.

For generously offering his linguistic and editorial

expertise in the preparation of this entire volume, I am once again in debt to John King. Chapter 5, "Fiction and Reality in Latin America," which he edited, is based on a lecture, "Latin America: Fiction and Reality," originally delivered in Edinburgh in 1986 and published in *On Modern Latin American Fiction* (New York: Farrar Straus & Giroux, 1989). Chapter 6, on Isaiah Berlin, was first published in much-abridged form in *Making Waves* (New York: Farrar Straus & Giroux, 1997), a collection of my essays edited and translated by John King. He also translated part of Chapter 7, on Karl Popper, which is a much-expanded and revised version of an essay published in *PMLA* (October 1990) and translated by Jonathan Titler of Cornell University, to whom I am also grateful. And finally, my very special thanks to Susan Wallace Boehmer of Harvard University Press for her intelligent suggestions concerning the organization of the book and for the care with which she edited the chapters and helped to polish them.